Nelson

ENGLISH

SKILLS

BOOK 5

JOHN JACKMAN
WENDY WREN

Nelson

Contents

Vocabulary	Punctuation/ Grammar	Spelling	Quiz
acronyms	parts of speech	Tips for better spelling 1: 'e' + suffix	word order
gender words	commas, possessive adjectives, articles	Tips for better spelling 2: 'ery'/ 'ary' endings	homophones
conversation words	direct and indirect speech	Tips for better spelling 3: 'our' + 'ous' suffix	anagrams
building words	paragraphs	Tips for better spelling 4: 'll' + prefix or suffix	dictionary guide words
either/or neither/nor	making new verbs choosing adjectives abbreviations	Tips for better spelling 5: consonant doubling	word game
dictionary work metaphors	abstract nouns	Tips for better spelling 6: 'able' / 'ible' endings	vowel deletion game
redundant words	punctuation marks relative pronouns	Tips for better spelling 7: 'y' + suffix	word game
words change	verbs: active and passive	Tips for better spelling 8: making plurals	word game
prefixes	types of clause: main/subordinate	Fifteen tricky words	punctuation puzzle
alliteration, onomatopoeia, word repetition, synonyms and idioms	direct speech punctuation marks	Tips for better spelling 9: 'f' and 'fe' plurals	common errors puzzle
synonyms and eponyms	colons using auxiliary verbs	Tips for better spelling 10: 'o' plurals	religious research activity
using a thesaurus improving sentences	expanding sentences adding words, phrases and clauses	Thirty tricky words	odd one out
puns	abstract nouns, idioms/ suffixes, parts of speech	Tips for better spelling 11: 'i' before 'e'	missing words
definitions word webs	personal letter formal (business) letter	Tips for better spelling 12: adding prefixes	antonyms and synonyms
collective nouns	types of sentence: simple/compound	Another thirty tricky words	cat/dictionary quiz

UNIT 1

City life

Changing Times

Many things are changing
Today in London Town
New buildings going up
Old ones coming down
Just like London people
Houses too grow old
And can no longer do their job
To keep out damp and cold
Many are old fashioned
And were built long ago
For people in a different age
Who didn't hurry so
People's ways are changing
Like the things we use
Telephones for speaking
Television news
Just try to imagine
How things used to be
Different songs to listen to
Different things to see
Everyone used horses
Or else their own two feet
Everything moved slowly
Like the policeman on his beat
No motor cars to take them
Quickly on their way
No discos or videos
Like there are today
No package holidays
And no aeroplanes
No electric railways
And only puffer trains
People used to manage
It didn't matter how
But when you come to think of it
Aren't you glad it's NOW.

Eric Slayter

Piccadilly Circus in the 1890s

Piccadilly Circus in the 1990s

COMPREHENSION

A Make lists of words or phrases that would make sense in each of the gaps in this paragraph. For some gaps you may be able to think of several possibilities. Draw a neat line under the word in each list which you would choose to use.

Towns and cities have changed __1__ in the last 100 years. It is now __2__ easier for people to __3__ to work using __4__, which means they can __5__ farther away. Also, travel by __6__ has meant that some people can take holidays in __7__ places. Some forms of entertainment, such as __8__, which are popular now, weren't even invented in the 1890s.

Our Street

Our street is not a posh place,
Say the mums in curlers, dads in braces, kids in nothing.
Our street is not a quiet place,
Says the football match, our honking bikes, our shouts.
Our street is not a tidy place,
Say the lolly wrapper, chippie bags, and written-on walls.
Our street is not a lazy place,
Say the car washing dads, clothes washing mums, and marbling boys.
Our street is not a new place,
Say the paint-peeled doors, pavements worn, and crumbly walls.
Our street is not a green place,
Say the pavements grey, forgotten gardens, lines of cars.
But our street is the best
Says me.

L. T. Baynton

COMPREHENSION

B Read the poem and study the picture.

1 Make two lists – one of the ways in which the street in the poem is similar to where you live, and another of all the differences between your home area and 'Our Street'.

2 Would you like to live in 'Our Street'? Give your reasons.

3 Imagine that you are an elderly person. Write about all the advantages and then all the disadvantages of living in 'Our Street'.

VOCABULARY

Acronyms

An **acronym** is a word made from the first letters of a series of other words.

Example: Posh **P**ort **o**ut **s**tarboard **h**ome

(In the days when most journeys to India and beyond were by ship, the best cabins were away from the direct sun; you needed to be on the port side going out and on the starboard side coming home. The passengers who could afford to pay more for these cabins were called the **posh** people.)

A Use a dictionary or other reference books to discover what these acronyms mean.

1 RoSPA 2 OXFAM 3 UNESCO
4 UNICEF 5 NATO 6 RAF

GRAMMAR

Parts of speech

There are eight main **parts of speech** into which words can be divided, depending on the work they do in a sentence.

Part of speech	Description	Example
noun	a naming word	telephone London
pronoun	takes the place of a noun	they he it me
adjective	describes a noun or pronoun	green small
verb	an action or doing word a being word	came spoke was be am
adverb	describes the action of a verb	slowly tomorrow
conjunction	a joining word	and but until
interjection	an exclamation	oh! ouch!
preposition	shows the relationship between two things or people	on for in

A Copy the words in *italics*. Next to each word, state what part of speech it is in its sentence.

1 The *tall policeman* was walking *his* beat.

2 He *ran quickly* to where *he heard* the noise.

3 The *small girls were screaming and* a *toddler was crying.*

4 Other *children* who *live in* the *street gathered around.*

5 "*Ouch*!" *cried* the *girl* as the *policeman lifted her off* the *road.*

6 *She was certainly hurt*, *but* not *badly*.

B Read the poems on pages 4 and 6 again, and from them make a list of four nouns, four verbs, four adjectives, four pronouns and four prepositions.

> Some words can be used in more than one way, and so can be used as more than one **part of speech**.
>
> *Example:* The area a policeman patrols is called his **beat**. (*noun*)
>
> John **beat** Peter by ten points in the spelling competition. (*verb*)

C Write out the words in the box that can be used as nouns or as verbs. Write sentences for three of the words, using them as both nouns and verbs in the same sentence.

tie	fire	rule	lolly	Wales	fly	lift

SPELLING

Tips for better spelling: 1

A suffix is a word ending.

To add a suffix when a word ends with **e**:

drop the **e** if the suffix begins with a **vowel**
Examples: wake/waking shame/shamed

keep the **e** if the suffix begins with a **consonant**
Examples: wake/wakeful shame/shameful

Some exceptions: true/truly, argue/argument, due/duly

A Add these suffixes to each of the words. Write the new word that is formed.

1	package + ing	2	place + ed	3	state + ment
4	argue + ing	5	combine + ation	6	safe + ty
7	relate + ion	8	base + ment	9	imagine + ation
10	insure + ance	11	care + less	12	share + ing

QUIZ

Ploughman's challenge

This is a line from a poem by Thomas Gray.

The ploughman homeward plods his weary way.

How many different ways can you arrange these seven words to make a sentence?

You must use all seven words each time, but the sentence need not end up meaning the same thing.

Here is one to get you started.

Homeward the weary ploughman plods his way.

UNIT 2

London life in Victorian times

By the time they had turned into the Bethnal Green Road, the day had fairly begun to break. Many of the lamps were already extinguished; a few country waggons were slowly toiling on, towards London; now and then, a stage coach, covered with mud, rattled briskly by . . . The public houses, with gas lights burning inside, were already open. By degrees, other shops began to be unclosed, and a few scattered people were met with.

Then, came straggling groups of labourers going to their work; then, men and women with fish baskets on their heads; donkey carts laden with vegetables; chaise carts filled with livestock or whole carcasses of meat; milk women with pails . . . As they approached the City, the noise and traffic gradually increased; when they threaded the streets between Shoreditch and Smithfield, it had swelled into a roar of sound and bustle. It was as light as it was likely to be, till night came on again, and the busy morning of half the London population had begun . . .

It was market morning. The ground was covered, nearly ankle-deep, with filth and mire; . . . the fog, which seemed to rest upon the chimney tops, hung heavily above. All the pens in the centre of the large area, and as many temporary pens as could be crowded into the vacant space, were filled with sheep; tied up to posts by the gutter side were long lines of beasts and oxen, three or four deep. Countrymen, butchers, drovers, hawkers, boys, thieves, idlers, and vagabonds of every low grade, were mingled together in a mass; the whistling of drovers, the barking of dogs, the bellowing and plunging of oxen, the bleating of sheep, the grunting and squeaking of pigs, the cries of hawkers, the shouts, oaths, and quarrelling on all sides; the ringing of bells and roar of voices, that issued from every public house; the crowding, pushing, driving, beating, whooping, and yelling; the hideous and discordant din that resounded from every corner of the market; and the unwashed, unshaven, squalid, and dirty figures constantly running to and fro, and bursting in and out of the throng; rendered it a stunning and bewildering scene, which quite confounded the senses . . .

'Now, young un!' said Sikes, looking up at the clock of St Andrew's Church, 'hard upon seven! you must step out. Come, don't lag behind already, Lazylegs!'

Mr Sikes accompanied this speech with a jerk at his little companion's wrist; Oliver, quickening his pace into a kind of trot, between a fast walk and a run, kept up with the rapid strides of the housebreaker as well as he could.

They held their course at this rate, until they had passed Hyde Park corner, and were on their way to Kensington: when Sikes relaxed his pace, until an empty cart which was at some little distance behind, came up. Seeing 'Hounslow' written on it, he asked the driver with as much civility as he could assume, if he would give them a lift as far as Isleworth.

'Jump up,' said the man. 'Is that your boy?'

'Yes; he's my boy,' replied Sikes, looking hard at Oliver, and putting his hand abstractedly into the pocket where the pistol was.

'Your father walks rather too quick for you, don't he, my man?' inquired the driver: seeing that Oliver was out of breath.

'Not a bit of it,' replied Sikes, interposing. 'He's used to it. Here, take hold of my hand, Ned. In with you!'

Thus addressing Oliver, he helped him into the cart; and the driver, pointing to a heap of sacks, told him to lie down there, and rest himself.

Extracts from *Oliver Twist*, written by Charles Dickens in 1839

COMPREHENSION

A Write a sentence to answer each question.

1. What form of lighting was used in public houses?
2. Why were there so many animals in the street?
3. At what time did Oliver and Sikes pass St Andrew's Church?
4. Where were the two heading?
5. How did the cart-driver realise Oliver was finding it difficult to keep up with Sikes?

B

1. Write a short paragraph to describe either Oliver or Sikes. Don't forget to describe the character's personality as well as what he looked like.
2. Think of possible reasons why Sikes may have been carrying a pistol in his pocket.
3. Find these short passages and then write them in your own words. Use a dictionary to help you.
   - **a** the day had fairly begun to break
   - **b** By degrees, other shops began to be unclosed
   - **c** the hideous and discordant din
   - **d** with as much civility as he could assume

VOCABULARY

Gender words

Remember, **gender** words tell whether something is:

masculine (male)	*Examples:* boy his bull
feminine (female)	*Examples:* women hers hen
common (*either* male *or* female)	*Examples:* Victorians dogs they
neuter (*neither* male *nor* female)	*Examples:* church clock cart

A Write the words of the opposite gender to these.

1	girl	2	father	3	woman	4	bridegroom
5	him	6	husband	7	daughter	8	she
9	cow	10	king	11	drake	12	Mr

Remember, **pronouns** (like *him*, *it*, *they*) are used in place of **nouns**.

B Make four lists, headed **masculine**, **feminine**, **common**, **neuter**. Read the passage on pages 10–12 again to find four nouns and four pronouns for each list. If you can't find enough in the passage for all the lists, add some others of your own choice.

PUNCTUATION

Using commas in sentences

We use *and* or *or* before the final item in a list.

We use **commas** between items in a list or between groups of words (though not normally before **or** or **and**).

Example: Victorians would not have known about television, videos, spacecraft or package holidays.

We use **commas** between the parts of a sentence to help the reader know where to make a short pause.

Examples: The idea of sending postcards, which came from Austria, became very popular in Victorian times.
Yes, I like sweets.
Oliver had a tough life, didn't he?

We use **commas** to separate the actual words spoken in direct speech from the rest of the sentence.

Example: "Jump up," said the man.

A Add commas where needed in these sentences.

1. Countrymen butchers drovers hawkers boys thieves idlers and vagabonds were mingled together.
2. The whistling of drovers the barking of dogs the bellowing of oxen and the bleating of sheep resounded from every corner of the market.
3. The public houses with gas lights burning inside were already open.
4. Oliver quickening his pace into a trot did his best to keep up.
5. "Yes he's my boy" replied Sikes looking hard at Oliver.

GRAMMAR

Possessive adjectives

Adjectives are sometimes called 'describing' words because they tell us more about nouns.

my your his her its our their

These are called **possessive** adjectives because they tell us who owns or *possesses* something. *Example:* That is **my** hat.

Be careful! **Possessive adjectives** *describe* a noun.
Example: That is **my** hat.

Possessive pronouns *stand in place of* a possessive adjective and a noun. *Example:* That is **mine** (= my hat).

A Write out a possessive adjective which could fill the gap in each of these sentences.

1 Dad and ____ friends worked in a factory.
2 They were always pleased when ____ factory closed for a day.
3 ____ mum and dad didn't have much money.
4 Mum said that ____ parents never went on a train.
5 The steam train blew ____ whistle loudly.
6 "Harold, are these ____ dirty old trousers?" asked his wife.

Articles

Articles are the three short words **a, an** and **the**.

Not many people know that these are adjectives!

A Copy this short passage, neatly underlining the articles in red, the possessive adjectives in blue and any other adjectives in green.

A small, wizened old lady asked my mother if she could tell our fortunes. "Your fortune telling doesn't work!" said Mum. "Last time you looked in the glass ball you said that our scraggy old dog would have five pups, that my sore knee would stop hurting, and that an old red hen we keep would stop laying its eggs. None of these things happened, so your fortune telling is a waste of my time."

SPELLING

Tips for better spelling: 2

Most words that end in **ary** are adjectives (descriptions), or people. *Examples:* imagin**ary** mission**ary**

Most words that end in **ery** are nouns (things or places)
Examples: machin**ery** bak**ery**
or adjectives made from words that end in **er**.
Examples: thunder thund**ery**; powder powd**ery**

A Copy these words carefully, just as they are set out here.

			B	A	K						
	T	H	U	N	D						
		M	O	N	A	S	T				
M	I	S	S	I	O	N					
		R	E	V	O	L	U	T	I	O	N
	C	E	M	E	T						
		B	U	R	G	L					
				S	I	L	V				
		S	T	A	T	I	O	N			
			D	R	A	P					
			D	Y	S	E	N	T			

1 Fill in the missing **ary** or **ery** endings.

2 Find a word which runs vertically, meaning an annual celebration.

3 One of the words can have either an **ary** or an **ery** ending. Which is it? Write a sentence for each ending, showing that you know the difference in meaning which corresponds to the different spellings.

QUIZ

Homophone puzzle

Homophones are words with the same sound but a different spelling and meaning.

Examples: Beatrice *rode* her horse along the *road*.
It was difficult to see the *knight* at *night*.

Which homophones do each of these pictures remind you of?

A B C D

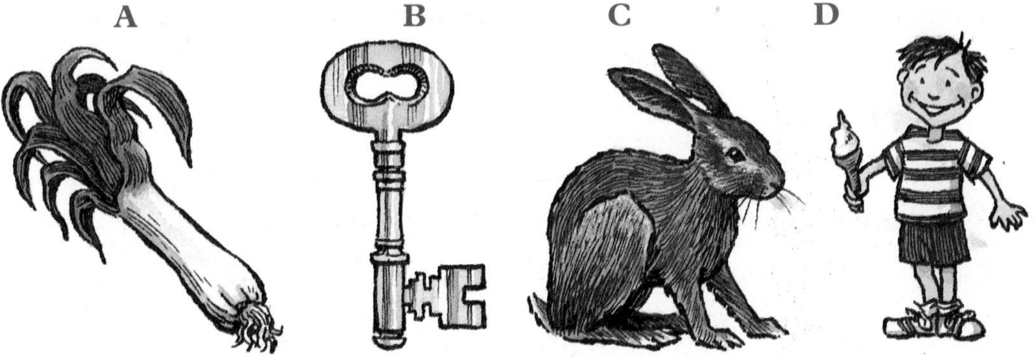

Here are some more difficult **homophones**. Use your dictionary to check what each word means and use it in a sentence.

current currant faint feint lightening lightning

Centaurus I

by Jack Richards and James Feldman

Cast
Narrator 1 also plays Mr Sotelo
Narrator 2 also plays Voice on Tape
Grant Carter: Crew member
Michelle Carter: Crew member
Don Chan: Crew member; also plays Mr Chan
Margaret Chan: Crew member
John Fermi: Captain
Pauline Sotelo: Crew member
Peter Bibikov: Executive Officer; also plays Mr Bibikov

Narrator 1: In the year 2000, the spaceship *Centaurus I* left Earth and headed for its nearest galactic neighbour, Centaurus Proxima. Problems on Earth had grown so great that many people doubted man's ability to survive . . .

Centaurus I is provided with all things needed to educate, feed, and entertain a crew numbering 100. The present generation – the 17th – has lost identification with its ancestors, as well as with the original purpose of the trip. To the people aboard, the ship has become their world. The closer they come to their destination, the more unbearable becomes the thought of giving up their security for an alien life.

Narrator 2: It is now October, 2492. You are on the earthship *Centaurus I*, which is 492 years away from Earth on its journey to the solar system of Centaurus Proxima. As the play opens, some members of the crew are involved in a serious conversation.

Grant: (*Loudly*) I've said it again and again. We must go back before it's too late.

Michelle: We'll never turn back as long as Captain Fermi is in command.

Don: I agree. He's impossible to reason with.

Grant: Then we'll not try to reason with him. We'll use force to take the ship from him . . . don't you know that tomorrow we reach PNR?

Margaret: What do you mean, PNR?

Grant: You've been aboard the ship all these years and haven't heard about the point of no return? Tomorrow at 1400 hours we reach that point in our journey from which there can be no turning back . . . At this time we come under the influence of the gravitational pull of Centaurus. Once that happens, we can never leave.

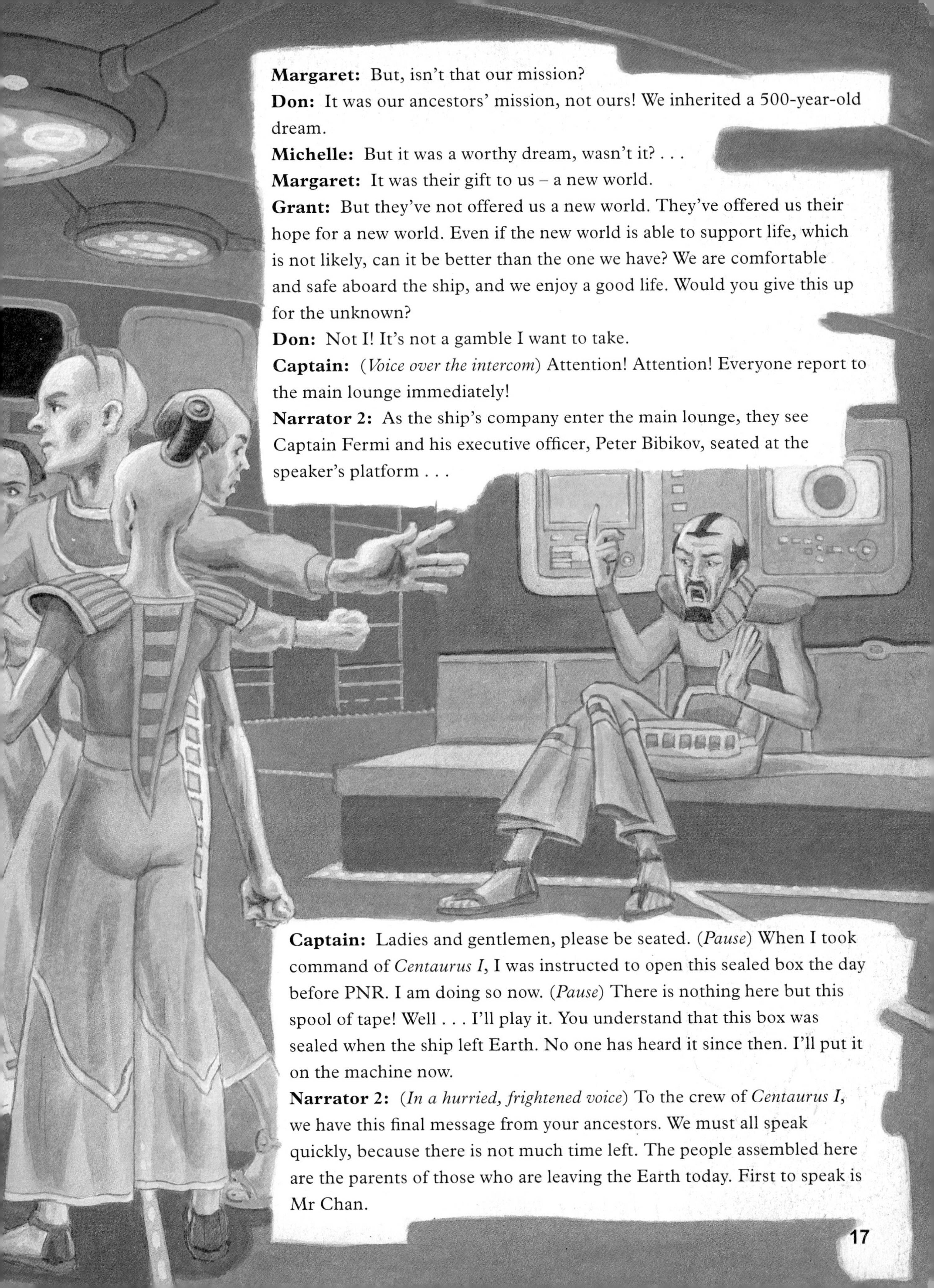

Margaret: But, isn't that our mission?
Don: It was our ancestors' mission, not ours! We inherited a 500-year-old dream.
Michelle: But it was a worthy dream, wasn't it? . . .
Margaret: It was their gift to us – a new world.
Grant: But they've not offered us a new world. They've offered us their hope for a new world. Even if the new world is able to support life, which is not likely, can it be better than the one we have? We are comfortable and safe aboard the ship, and we enjoy a good life. Would you give this up for the unknown?
Don: Not I! It's not a gamble I want to take.
Captain: (*Voice over the intercom*) Attention! Attention! Everyone report to the main lounge immediately!
Narrator 2: As the ship's company enter the main lounge, they see Captain Fermi and his executive officer, Peter Bibikov, seated at the speaker's platform . . .

Captain: Ladies and gentlemen, please be seated. (*Pause*) When I took command of *Centaurus I*, I was instructed to open this sealed box the day before PNR. I am doing so now. (*Pause*) There is nothing here but this spool of tape! Well . . . I'll play it. You understand that this box was sealed when the ship left Earth. No one has heard it since then. I'll put it on the machine now.
Narrator 2: (*In a hurried, frightened voice*) To the crew of *Centaurus I*, we have this final message from your ancestors. We must all speak quickly, because there is not much time left. The people assembled here are the parents of those who are leaving the Earth today. First to speak is Mr Chan.

Mr Chan: I am sending my son and my name into space because neither will continue here on Earth. Oh, please keep us alive on your new planet! Here we are starving. The world is overflowing with people. There is no room left to grow food. And that which we grow is taken from us by wild bands of starving humanity. Please, please keep life going!

Mr Bibikov: (*Hoarsely*) I am Dimitri Bibikov. As my son boards the ship, I can think only that he will breathe clean air for the first time in his life. Our planet is covered with black smoke. Our lives are a constant struggle against the filthy air. Our lungs are ruined. We are sick. May you find, wherever you go, air that will give you life, not hurry your death . . .

Captain: (*Shouting*) All aboard! Quickly!

Mr Sotelo: (*Shouting*) We are the last Sotelos on Earth! The Earth is finished! Life is over! Go quickly!

Narrator 2: (*Speaking hurriedly, but softly*) The Captain is waiting for this spool of tape. Ladies and gentlemen of the future, think of what you have just heard. You are being sent to keep mankind alive somewhere in the universe. When you hear this tape, you will be faced with the same awesome responsibility we are faced with today – to decide the fate of your descendants. May wisdom guide your thinking. Good-bye. God bless you. Good-bye from Earth.

Grant: Is that all?

Pauline: What else is there to say?

Grant: This still doesn't change anything.

Captain: As Captain of *Centaurus I*, it is my decision that we complete the mission our ancestors started.

Don: That's not your decision to make! That's a decision that should be made by all of us.

Crew: I agree! That's right! We all should decide! . . .

Pauline: Members of the crew: Let us not waste time arguing! We should at least respect the wishes of our ancestors and be guided by reason . . . Our position seems clear. To enter PNR means to commit our future generations to life in a new solar system – one that may or may not be able to support life. To return to Earth means life for another 500 years, perhaps, but still life without hope.

Don: What do you mean, life without hope? It had life for our ancestors. We have no reason to believe that life does not exist on Earth now. Surely they wouldn't be mad enough to blow up their planet!

Michelle: Not one answer to our many messages has been received from Earth during the lifetime of anyone aboard. Can we assume there is still life there?

Grant: Of course we can! Why should they continue to attempt to communicate with us? A message both ways now would take over eight years. They've probably forgotten us. They've had their problems. We just heard some of them.

Michelle: It's more reasonable to assume that they cannot communicate with us.

Grant: Enough of this! How many want to turn back?

Narrator: (*Facing and addressing the audience*) Well . . . what do we do?

COMPREHENSION

A Select one of the options from each box to complete these sentences correctly.

1 *Centaurus I* left Earth in [1900 / 2000 / 2492].

2 The captain's name is [Bibikov / Michelle / Fermi].

3 The crew listened to a message [on a radio / in a letter / on a tape].

4 It would take 8 [days / weeks / years] to get a message to Earth and back.

B Write a sentence to answer each question.

1 What does PNR stand for, and why is it important for the crew of *Centaurus I*?

2 Why did *Centaurus I* leave Earth in the first place?

3 Why are some members of the crew concerned about the future?

4 If you were on board the spaceship, what would you vote to do? What are your reasons?

VOCABULARY

Conversation words

The careful selection of expressive words adds to the quality of our writing. Here is a list of some of the many words which are alternatives to **said**.

warned	asked	yelled	retorted	answered	shouted
stammered	objected	inquired	sobbed	laughed	
squealed	cried	growled	remarked	urged	decided
replied	interrupted	whimpered	roared	grumbled	
mumbled	muttered	drawled	bellowed	whispered	
explained	exclaimed	continued	pleaded	called	

A Copy these sentences, choosing one of the words in the box as a more expressive alternative to **said**.

1 "We must go back before it's too late," said Grant.

2 "We'll never turn back as long as Captain Fermi is in command," said Michelle.

3 "I agree, it's impossible to reason with him," said Don.

4 "What do you mean, PNR?" said Margaret.

5 "Tomorrow we reach the point in our journey from which there is no turning back," said Grant.

6 "It was our ancestors' mission, not ours," said Don.

7 "The Earth is finished! Life is over! Go quickly!" said Mr Sotelo.

8 "Surely they wouldn't be mad enough to blow up their planet!" said Don.

9 "Enough of this! How many want to turn back?" said Grant.

GRAMMAR

Direct and indirect speech

Remember, **direct speech** is when you write *the actual words* that a person has spoken. We show this by putting **inverted commas** (" . . . ") around the spoken words.

Example: "What do you mean, PNR?" asked Margaret.

Indirect speech is when you *write about* (or *report*) what a person has said, without using the actual words spoken – so you don't need inverted commas.

Example: Margaret asked what he meant by PNR.

Indirect speech is sometimes called 'reported' speech.

A Write each of these sentences as indirect speech.

1. "What happens when we run short of fuel?" asked Don anxiously.
2. "That simply isn't possible," replied the Captain.
3. "What a ridiculous claim," shouted Grant, leaping to his feet.
4. "Be very careful what you say. I am in charge of this craft," warned Captain Fermi, "and I won't have insubordination."

B Convert each of these sentences to direct speech.

1. Michelle told Margaret that she thought Grant had said too much.
2. Don held Grant's arm and encouraged him to sit down.
3. Grant muttered to Don that time was running out.
4. Don reassured him that they were safer going on than trying to return to Earth.

SPELLING

Tips for better spelling: 3

To add the suffix **ous** or **ious** to most words ending with **our**, drop the **u** in the word to which the suffix is added.

Example: humour + ous = humorous

A Add **ous** or **ious** to each of these words. Write a sentence which shows the meaning of each of the new words that you have formed.

1 rigour 2 labour 3 vigour 4 vapour

QUIZ

Anagrams

Anagrams are words made by rearranging the letters of another word. How quickly can you solve these anagrams? The first is done for you.

ample	a type of tree	*maple*
paws	a stinging insect	
softer	where lots of trees grow	
earth	an important organ in the body	
solemn	large, round fruit	
groan	a large musical instrument	
disease	where we often go on holiday	

UNIT 4

Lilliput

One fine morning in May of the year 1699, young Doctor Lemuel Gulliver kissed his beloved wife and children farewell and eagerly boarded the sailing ship *Antelope* . . . Gulliver had always loved adventures, and when he was offered the position of ship's doctor he had accepted at once.

For many weeks all went well. But . . . a terrible storm arose. Battered by the wind and waves, the *Antelope* struck a rock, splintered and sank . . . What became of his shipmates he never found out, but Gulliver himself managed to swim to an island. Exhausted, he dragged himself up on the shore and fell instantly into a deep sleep. Let Gulliver tell you in his own words of the events that followed . . .

I must have slept for a long time, for the sun had risen and shone quite high overhead when I awoke. I tried to stand up but found to my astonishment that I could not move. My hands and feet and even my hair seemed to be fastened down. Then I was horrified to feel some small animal creeping along my left leg and up to my chest. Straining to lift my head a little, I peered down and saw a tiny human creature not much bigger than my own middle finger. He was followed by about forty more of the same kind.

I was so surprised that I roared aloud. At this, they all ran back in fright and some even tumbled off. However, they soon came back and one climbed up to where he could get a full sight of my face.

"Hekinah degul!" he called out but, although I have studied several other languages beside my native English, I could not understand these words at all.

With a violent pull, I managed to break a few of the strings that bound my left hand. I then tried to catch some of the annoying little creatures, but they ran away too quickly.

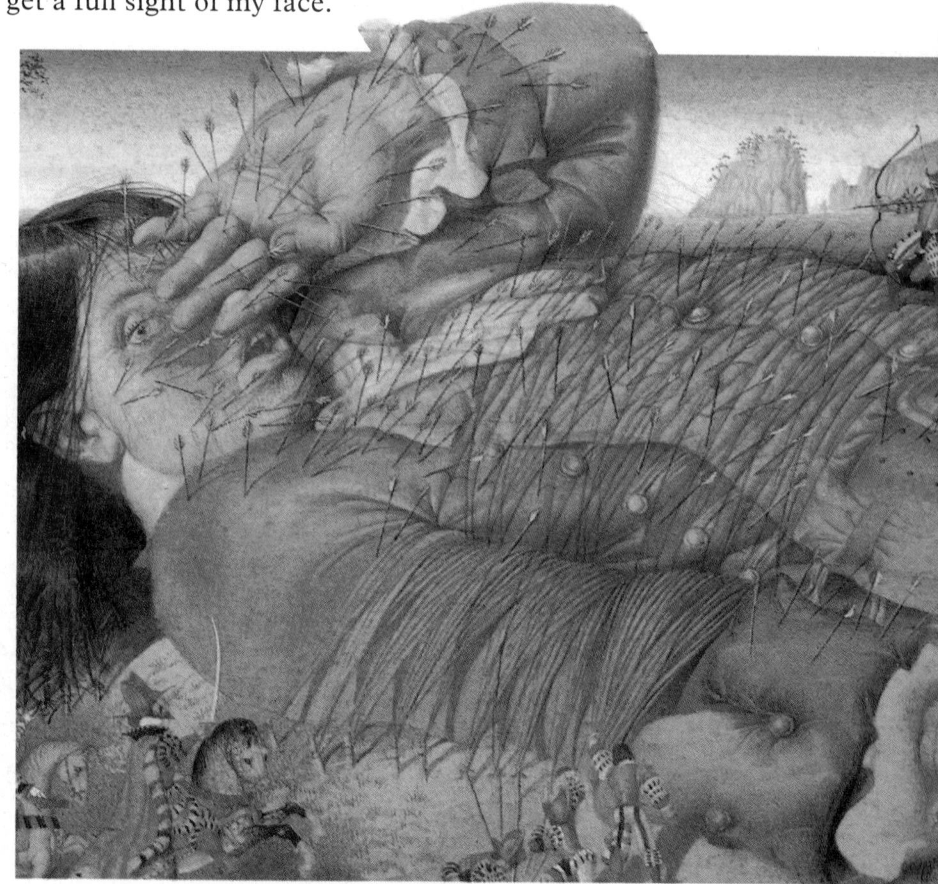

Then one of them cried out *"Tolgo phonac!"* In an instant I felt my left hand and my face pierced with hundreds of tiny arrows. I decided not to anger my small captors further. I lay still and tried to think about how to get them to set me free.

After a little while, I heard some knocking near my right ear and the sound of a great crowd. Turning my head as far as I could, I saw that some of the tiny people were building a tower about a foot and a half high. Now one little man, who seemed to be someone of importance, climbed up to the top of it and made a long speech, which I could not understand. He said the word *"Lilliput"* several times, however, and I guessed that this might be the name of the place I was in. He looked quite friendly and, since I was very hungry, I pointed to my mouth to indicate this.
Before long, about a hundred inhabitants set ladders against my sides and climbed up and walked toward my mouth, carrying little baskets of food: miniature legs of lamb, tiny roasted turkeys or sides of beef. They were deliciously cooked, but three of them together made scarcely a mouthful for me.

Then someone called out, *"Peplum selam."* At this, they loosened the cords that bound me a little, so I was able to turn on my side. Before I knew it I was fast asleep. Only later did I discover that their doctors had put a sleeping potion into my food.

From *Gulliver's Adventures in Lilliput* by Jonathan Swift,
retold by Ann Beneduce,

COMPREHENSION

A Copy the statements below that are true.

1 Gulliver was a ship's doctor.

2 He asked to be put ashore at Lilliput.

3 His ship was wrecked and he managed to swim to an island.

4 The island was populated by giants.

5 He was captured by a crowd of very small people.

6 Gulliver knew he must be on Lilliput by the tiny signpost.

7 About a hundred tiny people walked all over his outstretched body.

8 The miniature humans put the doctor to sleep by slipping a potion into his meal.

B Answer these questions with one or more sentences, as appropriate.

1 How did the tiny humans restrain Gulliver?

2 What were the first words he heard spoken on Lilliput?

3 Individually, the tiny folk could not have restrained Gulliver, but working together they did so very successfully. Make a list of four things that we humans can only achieve by working in teams or groups.

4 Imagine you are the size of a Lilliputian person. Look out of the window and imagine that you spot a giant-size person striding towards you. Write a list of adjectives to describe the giant.

VOCABULARY

Building words

Gulliver *slowly opened* his *eyes*. He *gradually* became aware of his *extraordinary surroundings*. He *seemed* to be *lying* on an *uncomfortable* and *unusually rocky* part of the shore. Then *suddenly* he was *horrified* by the *realisation* that he was *fastened* down.

This passage shows how important **prefixes** and **suffixes** are in our writing. Many antonyms (opposites) are made by adding prefixes, most plurals are made by adding a suffix, but many other new words can also be made by adding a prefix, a suffix or both.

Examples:

Word	*Add a prefix*	*Add a suffix*	*Add a prefix and a suffix*
happy	unhappy	happiness happily	unhappiness unhappily
honest	dishonest	honestly honesty	dishonestly dishonesty

A **prefix** is added at the front of a word. A **suffix** is added at the end.

A Copy the chart above, and add words which are built from:

1 kind 2 perfect 3 usual 4 possible 5 direct

Some words can have more than one suffix at the same time.
Example: foolishness = fool + ish + ness

B Copy these words. Underline the first suffix and draw a neat circle around the second suffix. The first one is done to help you.

1 celebration(s)	2 thoughtfully	3 actions
4 awakened	5 peacefulness	6 amazingly
7 frightening	8 thankfulness	9 powerlessness

C Select from the words in **B** to complete each of these sentences.

1 Gulliver was ____ by the tiny human creatures.

2 He was suddenly aware of his ____ .

3 It was a ____ situation in which to find oneself.

4 He lay still with a sense of ____ that at least he hadn't been drowned in the storm.

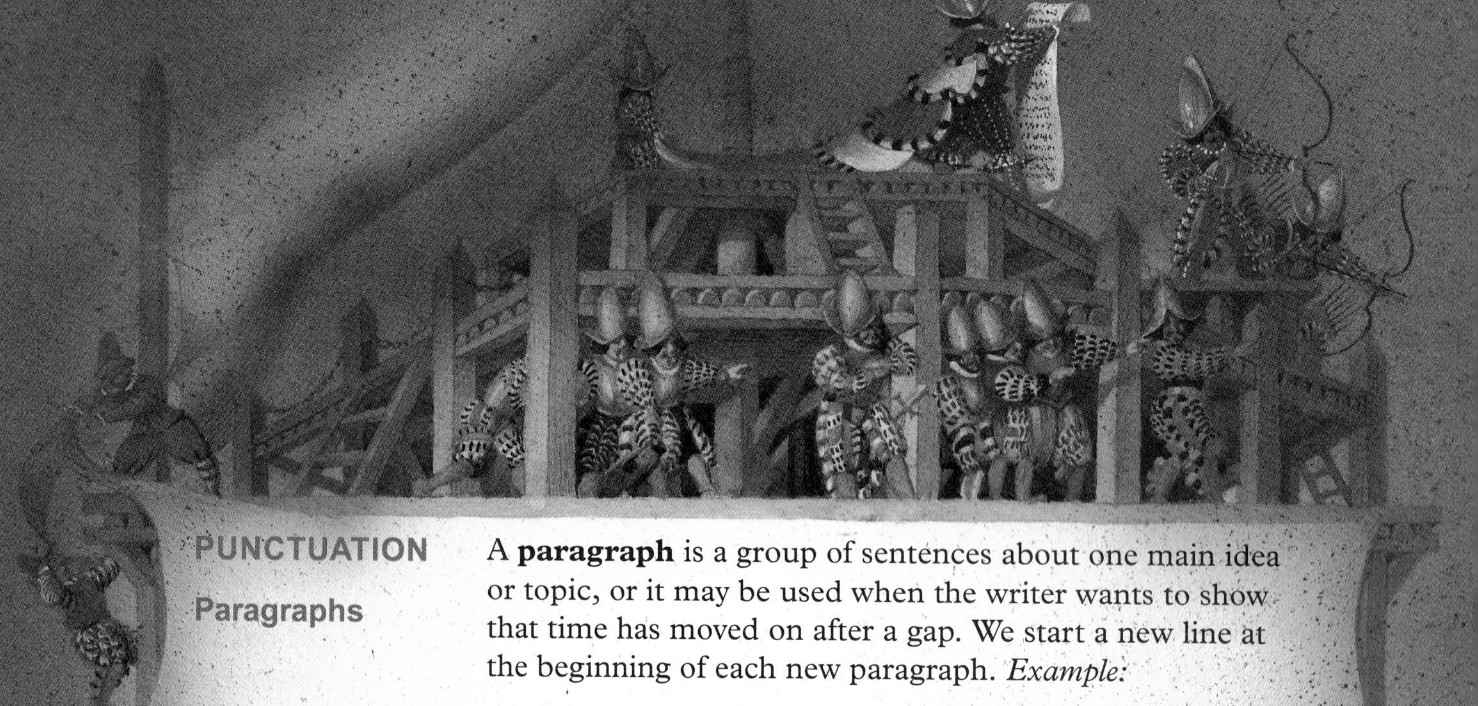

PUNCTUATION

Paragraphs

A **paragraph** is a group of sentences about one main idea or topic, or it may be used when the writer wants to show that time has moved on after a gap. We start a new line at the beginning of each new paragraph. *Example:*

> For many weeks all went well, until a terrible storm arose. Battered by the wind and waves, the *Antelope* struck a rock, splintered and sank. What became of his shipmates he never found out, but Gulliver himself managed to swim to an island. Exhausted, he dragged himself up on the shore and fell instantly into a deep sleep.

The **main idea** in this paragraph is:
Gulliver survived the storm and managed to reach the island.

A Look back at the extract and choose three of the paragraphs. Using not more than one sentence for each paragraph, describe the 'main ideas'.

B Choose one of the titles below. Write a short paragraph of four or five sentences to develop the topic. With a ruler, underline one sentence which summarises the 'main idea' of the paragraph.

A day I shall never forget — My favourite place — If I could have one wish come true

SPELLING

Tips for better spelling: 4

To add a prefix, a suffix or another word to most words ending with **ll** we drop one **l** from each **ll**.

Examples: will + full = wilful; skill + full = skilful
all + ways = always all + together = altogether

Be careful! There are several exceptions, especially words with a **ness** suffix.

Examples: smallness, stillness, dullness

A Join these together. Check your answers in a dictionary.

1 spoon + full	2 all + mighty	3 full + fill
4 full + ness	5 joy + full	6 fate + full
7 shrill + ness	8 hill + side	9 care + full

QUIZ

Dictionary guide words

A dictionary usually has **guide words** at the top of each page, showing the first and last words listed on that page or double-page spread. Make a list of the words in the box that would be on a page with ***indulge*** and ***inexhaustible*** as the guide words, and then put them in alphabetical order.

industrial inevitable infant indistinct inedible inequality inexplicable
industry inept inexhaustible ineffective individual inefficient

HOME SECRETARY 104 **HOSPITAL**

him realize.
to strike home to impress.
Home Secretary *n.* the government minister who deals with law and order in Britain.
homesick *adj.* longing to be home.
homespun *adj.* plain, made at home.
homeward *adj.* towards home.
homework *n.* work done at home.
honest *adj.* 1. never cheating or stealing. 2. truthful. *n.* **honesty** fair dealing.
honey *n.* sticky food made by bees. *n.* **honeycomb** rows of wax cells in which honey is stored.
honeymoon *n.* a newly wed couple's holiday.
honorary (*pron.* on'er.er.i) *adj.* 1. serving without pay, as *an honorary secretary receives no payment.* 2. (of a university degree) given as an honour, without passing examinations.
honour (*pron.* on'er) *n.* (spelt **honor** in the U.S.A.) 1. high regard, as *Mr Smith is held in honour.* 2. glory, fame, as *he did it for the honour of the school.* 3. honesty, fair dealing, as *he is a man of honour.* *adj.* **honourable** fair and honest.
Your Honour a title of respect, especially for a County Court judge.
hood *n.* 1. a covering for the head, usually attached to a coat. 2. a coloured top to a university gown. 3. a folding cover for a car or baby-carriage. 4. (in the U.S.A.) the bonnet of a motor-car. *adj.* **hooded**.
hoof *n.* the horny part of the foot of a horse or cow (*pl.* **hoofs** or **hooves**).
hook *n.* a bent piece of metal made to catch or hold something, as *a fish-hook or a curtain-hook.* *v.* **hook** to catch or fasten by a hook. *adj.* **hooked**.
hook-and-eye a hook and metal eye for fastening a dress.
by hook or by crook one way or another.
hooligan *n.* a ruffian. *n.* **hooliganism**.
hoop *n.* a wooden or metal ring for holding the staves of a barrel, for acrobats to jump through in a circus, etc.
hoot *v.* 1. to jeer. 2. to sound a motor-horn. 3. to make a noise like an owl. *n.* **hooter** a factory siren.
hooves see **hoof**.
hop (1) *n.* a trailing plant whose cones are used to flavour beer.
hop (2) *v.* to jump like a sparrow, or to jump on one leg (**hopping, hopped**). *n.* **hop** a short jump. *n.* **hopscotch** a hopping game.
hope *v.* to wish something will happen (**hoping, hoped**). *n.* **hope** 1. a wish. 2. confidence, as *we all have plenty of hope.* *adj.* **hopeful** expecting something with confidence. *adj.* **hopeless** without hope.
horde *n.* a crowd, a rabble.
horizon *n.* the line where earth and sky, or sea and sky, seem to meet.
horizontal *adj.* flat, parallel to the ground. *adv.* **horizontally.** *see* **vertical**.
horn *n.* 1. a hard pointed growth on the heads of cows, etc. 2. the substance of which this growth is made. 3. an animal's horn used for holding things, as *a powder-horn* or *drinking-horn.* 4. a musical wind-instrument. 5. a warning signal, as *a fog-horn* or *motor horn.* *adj.* **horned** having horns. *adj.* **horny** like horn.
the horns of a dilemma two equally unpleasant ways out of a difficulty.
hornet *n.* a large kind of wasp.
hornpipe *n.* a lively sailors' dance.
horrible *adj.* dreadful, awful. *adv.* **horribly**.
horrid *adj.* nasty, terrible.
horrify *v.* to fill with horror (**horrifying, horrified**).
horror *n.* fear, terror.
horse *n.* an animal used for riding and drawing loads (*fem.* **mare**).
to ride the high horse to be arrogant and aloof.
horsepower *n.* a unit of engine-power.
horticulture *n.* the study of gardening. *adj.* **horticultural**.
hose *n.* 1. stockings, socks. 2. a long flexible pipe for water.
hospitable *adj.* friendly and kind to guests.
hospital *n.* a building in which sick or

HOSPITALITY 105 **HUMILIATE**

injured people are cared for.
hospitality *n.* friendly and generous treatment of guests.
host (1) *n.* an army, a great crowd.
host (2) *n.* 1. anyone who entertains guests (*fem.* **hostess**). 2. an innkeeper.
Host (3) *n.* in the Roman Catholic church, the consecrated bread of the Mass.
hostage *n.* someone kept prisoner as a pledge until certain promises have been fulfilled.
hostel *n.* 1. a home for students. 2. a hiker's resting-place. 3. an inn.
hostess *feminine* of **host** (2).
hostile *adj.* unfriendly, war-like.
hostility *n.* enmity, warfare.
hot *adj.* 1. full of heat, as *hot water.* 2. full of passion, as *hot words.* 3. strong to taste, as *hot mustard* (*comparative* **hotter,** *superlative* **hottest**).
hot cross bun a bun marked with a cross, eaten on Good Friday.
in hot water in trouble.
hot-headed *adj.* rash.
hot-tempered *adj.* quick to take offence.
hotel *n.* a large building with many rooms for travellers and holidaymakers.
hound *n.* a hunting-dog. *v.* **hound** to chase and worry.
hour *n.* 1. sixty minutes or the twenty-fourth part of the day. 2. the time shown by a clock. *adj.* **hourly** every hour.
at the eleventh hour at the last moment.
hour-glass *n.* an instrument for measuring time, in which sand runs for an hour.
house *n.* 1. a building in which people live. 2. an inn, a *public house.* 3. a theatre audience, as *the play attracted a full house.* 4. a business firm. *v.* **house** (*pron.* howz) to provide house, to give shelter, to store (**housing, housed**).
house-boat *n.* a riverside boat to live in.
housebreaker *n.* a burglar.
housefly *n.* the common fly.
household *n.* all the people of a house.
householder *n.* a house-owner or tenant.
housekeeper *n.* a woman paid to manage a house.
housemaid *n.* a female servant in a house.
housewife *n.* the mistress of a house.
hove *past* of **heave**.
hovel *n.* a poor cottage, a hut.
hover *v.* to keep in the air over one spot, as *the helicopter hovered over the ship.*
hovercraft *n.* a vehicle without wheels travelling on land or water.
how *adv.* 1. in what way, as *how will he go?* 2. to what extent, as *how deep is it?* 3. in what condition, as *how are you?*
however *adv.* 1. in what way, as *however did he manage?* *conj.* **however** and yet, as *I feel sure, however I may be wrong.*
howl *n.* a long wailing cry.
hub *n.* 1. the centre of a wheel. 2. any centre, as *the city is a hub of activity.*
hubbub *n.* a noisy commotion.
huddle *n.* to press close together (**huddling, huddled**). *n.* **huddle** a close pack, a crowd.
hue *n.* a colour.
a hue and cry a loud shouting after someone who is being chased.
hug *v.* 1. to clasp close in the arms. 2. to keep close to, as *to hug the edge of a road* (**hugging, hugged**).
huge *adj.* enormous. *adv.* **hugely**.
hull *n.* a ship's frame.
hum *v.* 1. to make a noise like a bee. 2. to make a tune down the nose. 3. to bustle with activity, as *the village hummed with excitement* (**humming, hummed**). *n.* **hum** a buzzing sound.
human *adj.* belonging to mankind. *n.* **human** a man, woman, or child. *adv.* **humanly** in a human way, as *I will do what is humanly possible.*
humane *adj.* kind, merciful.
humanity *n.* 1. all people. 2. human kindness, as *show humanity to the suffering.*
humble *adj.* 1. meek, as *a humble man.* 2. small and poor, as *a humble cottage.* *v.* **humble** to make a proud person humble (**humbling, humbled**). *adv.* **humbly** modestly.
humbug *n.* 1. a fraud. 2. a kind of peppermint. *v.* **humbug** to deceive (**humbugging, humbugged**).
humiliate *v.* to cover with shame

The library puzzle

Thousands of new books are published each year. Books are written and published on every conceivable factual subject, and thousands of fiction books are written with themes ranging from adventure to romance and from history to science fiction.

How, then, can we possibly puzzle out where to find just the book we might be interested to browse through or read, or that might provide the information we are seeking?

Like all good detective work, our investigation needs to be systematic.

- STEP 1 Decide whether you are looking for **non-fiction** (facts/information) or do you want a good **fiction** book (stories/poetry etc)?
- STEP 2 Go to either the *non-fiction* or the *fiction* section of the library.

Non-fiction section

Most school and public libraries use a system for sorting and numbering their thousands of books which was invented more than a century ago by a famous American librarian, Melvil Dewey – and it is wonderfully simple.

All non-fiction books are put into one of ten main 'classes'. Each class is divided into ten sub-sections, called 'divisions', so altogether there are 100 divisions. Most libraries even divide these divisions into 1000 smaller sections, and these into even smaller sub-sections, by using decimal numbers, which is why this method of sorting books is called the *Dewey Decimal System*.

Here are the 'classes' which Melvil Dewey devised.

000–099	General reference books, including encyclopedias, dictionaries etc
100–199	Philosophy
200–299	Religions of the world
300–399	Social sciences, including law, transport, customs
400–499	Languages, including English and foreign languages
500–599	Sciences, including mathematics, astronomy, chemistry, physics, animals, birds
600–699	Technology, including medicine, engineering, farming, building and homes
700–799	The arts, including painting, drawing, music, sport
800–899	Literature, including plays, poetry
900–999	Geography and history, including travel

If we were looking for a book that would give us information about birds, we would go to the 'class' on sciences, which is 500–599. This section is divided into 'divisions', like this:

500 pure sciences	550 geology
510 mathematics	560 fossils
520 astronomy	570 biology
530 physics	580 botany
540 chemistry	590 zoology

If we then look at division 590 (zoology) we find that it is divided into sub-divisions, and that one of these sub-divisions, number 598, has all the books on reptiles and birds.

Very quickly, therefore, we can target the few books that might be helpful and which will, with luck, contain the information we need.

COMPREHENSION

A Write a sentence to answer each question.

1 Most libraries are divided into two main sections. What are they?

2 Who invented the system for numbering non-fiction books, and what is it called?

B In which 'class' would you look for information books on each of these subjects? Answer by giving a range of numbers.

1 Buddha	2 wild flowers	3 ships
4 sheep farming	5 football	6 sketching
7 bridges	8 King George V	9 deserts
10 Shakespeare	11 Mozart	12 hospitals

C Looking in more detail at the science classification (500–599), what number divisions would you go to for these books? Use your dictionary if you need help.

1 Britain's Wild Flowers	2 Our Solar System
3 Geometry for Beginners	4 Gravity and Other Forces
5 Newts and Lizards	6 Scottish Rocks and Minerals

Fiction section

Unlike non-fiction books, the fiction titles are sometimes arranged on the shelves of the library in sections such as science fiction, crime or mystery. The books are arranged alphabetically by their authors' surnames, so as with the non-fiction books, you can quickly locate the particular books you may want to look at.

In some libraries, the author catalogue for the fiction books is kept on cards, usually in drawers, labelled as in the picture.

- STEP 3 What to do if the book you want isn't there.

Someone else may have been looking for the same book as you and so may have borrowed it from the shelf before you arrived. You can discover this by asking the librarian to check the catalogue. Either a record card or a computer record is kept for each book. This should show whether the library normally has the book you need and whether it is out on loan already.

COMPREHENSION

A In which drawer would you expect to find details of the books by each of these authors that the library keeps?

1 Leon Garfield	2 Joan Aitken	3 Roald Dahl
4 E Nesbit	5 Rudyard Kipling	6 Lewis Carroll
7 J R R Tolkien	8 Kenneth Grahame	9 T H White

B 1 How are fiction books organised on the shelves of your local library?

2 Why do you think that fiction books are arranged differently from the non-fiction books?

VOCABULARY

Either/or
Neither/nor

Either and **or** belong together, and **neither** and **nor** belong together; the pairs should not be mixed.

Examples: **Either** you **or** I must collect our books today.
They had **neither** yours **nor** mine when I called yesterday.

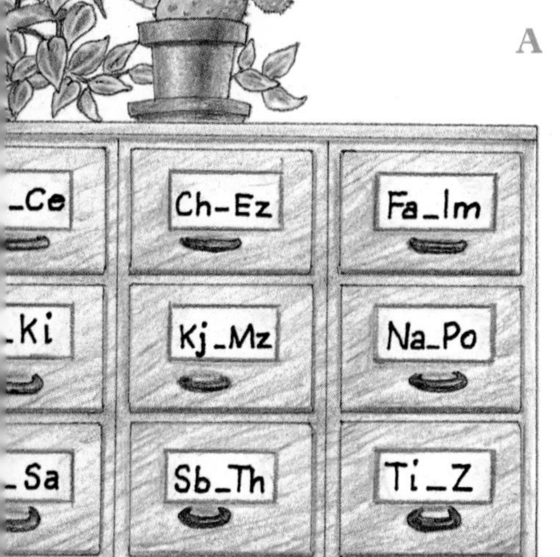

A Copy these sentences, filling the gaps with **either** and **or**, or **neither** and **nor**.

1. You can read about dinosaurs ____ in this book ____ in the encyclopedia.
2. ____ the school library ____ the public library had a copy of the book I needed.
3. ____ James ____ Matthew liked *The Railway Children*.
4. I don't mind, ____ I'll read it first ____ you can read it first.
5. It was ____ Ali ____ Manny, ____ it may even have been Danny, who borrowed the book last.

GRAMMAR

Making new verbs

Many simple, common verbs change their meanings depending on the preposition or adverb linked to them.

Example: put on   put off   put back   put out

I was **put off** the book by the dreary illustrations.

A Put each of these into short sentences which show their meaning.

1 take in   2 take up   3 take off   4 take away
5 take upon   6 take out   7 take over   8 take after

B How many different meanings can you create for each of these verbs by adding different prepositions or adverbs?
Write them out.

1 get   2 make   3 talk   4 put   5 run

Choosing adjectives

One of the most important reference books for a writer is a **thesaurus**, a book that lists words with similar meanings. Often, many alternatives are suggested, but only one might be just right for the occasion. Think carefully whether you need a **stronger**, a **weaker** or a **more accurate** word.

Example: In the *Nelson Concise Thesaurus*, the following alternatives are offered for **great**:

big large huge vast immense gigantic

A Write four sentences, each using a different synonym for **great**, taken from the box.

B Choose an adjective for each of the following contexts which is more suitable than the one shown. Your thesaurus will help you.

1 a drink you dislike *nasty*

2 a meal that is more than you can eat *big*

3 marshy land *wet*

4 an angry farmer *cross*

5 the winning team *pleased*

6 a storm at sea *rough*

Thesaurus comes from the Greek word for 'treasure'.

PUNCTUATION

Abbreviations

A Write the abbreviations for these terms.

1 Doctor
2 Her Majesty
3 Prime Minister
4 Police Constable
5 Independent Television
6 Member of Parliament

B You may need to do some research in reference books to find the full word or words (and sometimes the meaning) for each of these abbreviations.

1 BST 2 e.g. 3 pm 4 PTO 5 RSPCA
6 phone 7 BR 8 BSc 9 fridge 10 IOU

SPELLING

Tips for better spelling: 5

Remember, words can be divided into **syllables**. A syllable is a part of a word that has its own vowel sound.

When we say words, we emphasise, or **stress**, some syllables more than others.

Say these two words to yourself. Both have two syllables.

transmit = trans/mit **limit = lim/it**

When we say 'transmit' we **stress** 'mit', the second syllable; but when we say 'limit' we stress 'lim', the first syllable.

A Copy these words and draw a line after each syllable, if there is more than one. Underline the words whose last, or only, syllable is **stressed**.

1 dig 2 omit 3 hop 4 comic 5 public
6 transmit 7 itself 8 limit 9 profit 10 propel

When adding a suffix to a short word, or one whose last syllable is stressed, look at the letter before the last.

If the letter before the last is a single vowel (a,e,i,o,u), we usually **double the last letter before adding the suffix**.

Examples: h**o**p/hopping/hopped
omit/omitting (last syllable is stressed)
transmit/transmitted (last syllable is stressed)
propel/propelling (last syllable is stressed)

If the letter before the last is **not** a **single** vowel, or the last syllable is unstressed, we usually **just add the suffix**.

Examples: si**n**g/singing
r**ea**d/reading
profit/profited (last syllable is *not* stressed)

This tip doesn't work for words ending with **w**, **x** or **y**, which are *never* doubled.

Examples: box/boxed/boxing
mow/mowed/mowing

B Copy and complete this table. First, underline the stressed syllables and circle the second-last letters.

	add **ing**	add **ed**
admit	admitting	admitted
resist		
target		
benefit		
suggest		
dismiss		
borrow		

QUIZ

Sporting challenge

Each of these is a well-known sport. The only problem is that the printer has missed out all the consonants! Write them in.

1 __ __ i __ __ e __
2 __ __ i __ __ i __ __
3 __ o o __ __ a __ __
4 __ u __ __ __
5 __ __ o o __ e __
6 __ o __ __ e __
7 __ o __ __
8 __ e __ __ i __

Check-up 1

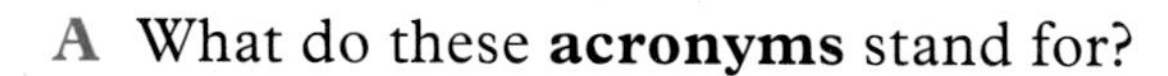

VOCABULARY

A What do these **acronyms** stand for?

1 UNICEF 2 OXFAM 3 RoSPA

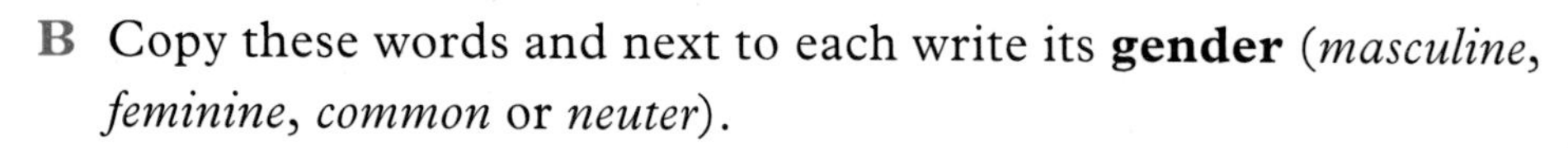

B Copy these words and next to each write its **gender** (*masculine, feminine, common* or *neuter*).

1 grandmother 2 uncle 3 Belfast 4 elephant
5 computer 6 Jenny 7 people 8 monk

C Add a **suffix** *and* a **prefix** to each of these words.

1 wake 2 honest 3 perfect 4 appoint

D Choose from the following words to fill the gaps in this short passage: **either or neither nor**.

I knew I had lent my games disk ____ to Ashok ____ to Suzie, but ____ of them could remember. ____ Ashok ____ Suzie will borrow my computer disks in future!

E Choose a better word than *said* to use in each of these sentences.

1 "I know I didn't borrow your disk!" said Suzie.
2 "What makes you think it was me?" said Ashok.
3 "I am absolutely sure it was one of you," I said.

PUNCTUATION

A Rewrite these sentences, changing those in **direct speech** into **indirect speech**, and those in **indirect speech** into **direct speech**.

1 Our teacher asked us if we would like to start a computer club at lunchtimes.
2 "How often would the club meet?" I asked her.
3 She thought we could meet about twice a week.
4 "I'm certain," I said, "that the club would be very popular."

B Rewrite this passage, adding the missing capital letters and punctuation marks.

miss jenkins our teacher suggested that we call the club the campbeltown school computer club she said we should make posters to advertise the first meeting owen ben maxine janie and i drew five posters we asked mrs smith if we could put them on the head teachers notice board

GRAMMAR

A Copy the words in *italics*, and next to each word write the **part of speech** it is in this sentence.

The *younger pupils watched intently* as *we explained carefully* how the *smart new computers worked.*

B Copy these sentences and add a suitable **possessive adjective** where necessary.

1 Several children brought ____ games.

2 May I borrow ____ computer?

3 What is ____ capacity?

4 It has a larger memory than ____ machine.

C Use three of these **abbreviations** in short sentences to show what they mean.

RSPCA PTO IOU pm MP Dr

SPELLING

A Add the **suffix** given to each of these words.

1 argue + ment	2 argue + ing	3 safe + ly
4 share + ed	5 care + ing	6 care + less
7 humour +ous	8 vigour + ous	9 begin + ing
10 transmit + ed	11 box + ing	12 sing + ing

B Each of these words ends with **ary** or **ery**. Write the words correctly.

1 imagin____	2 bak____	3 confection____
4 thund____	5 monast____	6 machin____
7 cemet____	8 station____	

9 One of these words can be spelt either way. Which one is it and what do the two words mean?

UNIT 6

The watery planet

'The Great Wave' by Hokusai, by courtesy of the Board of Trustees of the Victoria & Albert Museum

Of all the planets in our solar system only one, Earth, has water. There are two main reasons why there is water on Earth and not on the other planets. First, the appropriate chemicals are present on Earth to create water, namely hydrogen and oxygen; and secondly, we are just the right distance from the sun. If the Earth was closer to the sun the water in the seas and oceans would boil, but if Earth were further away, the water would all freeze.

Exactly how the oceans were originally formed remains something of a mystery, but what is certain is that nearly three-quarters of the surface of the Earth is now covered by water. Some scientists believe that Earth was once a ball of fire, and as it cooled, the rocks at the centre, which remained very hot, let off steam. This condensed into water as it escaped into the cold atmosphere, just as steam in a kitchen condenses into water droplets on a cold window.

Others think it is more probable that the water came from dense clouds which formed round the Earth. These clouds caused torrential rainstorms which lasted for thousands of years. As the rain fell on the higher land it washed salts from the rocks and flowed into the depressions on the planet's surface to form seas and oceans of salty water.

Fact File

- If all the salt in the oceans could be removed, it could be piled about 300 metres high on every part of the land surface of Earth, that is, about the height of the Eiffel Tower in Paris.
- The largest ocean, the Pacific, covers 63.8 million square miles (165 million square kilometres), which is nearly the same as all the other oceans on Earth put together.
- Beneath the oceans are mountain ranges longer and taller than any we see on land. The tallest mountain on Earth (from its base to its peak) is Mauna Kea on the island of Hawaii. It is 10,203 metres, although most is below the sea and only 4205 metres lies above sea level. This compares with Mount Everest, the tallest mountain on land, which is 8848 metres high.
- The Pacific Ocean was named by the explorer Magellan. Pacific means 'peaceful', but many who have experienced its storms and huge waves might question the appropriateness of this name.
- The Atlantic Ocean is the second-largest body of water on Earth. It has an enormous submerged mountain range running down its centre. Some people have associated this with the lost city of Atlantis, saying that at one time these mountain tops formed islands which supported a now lost civilisation.
- The Indian Ocean is about half the size of the Pacific, and is warmer and rather shallower. Nevertheless, its average depth is about 3800 metres!
- The Arctic Ocean, in many ways the most fascinating and mysterious of all the oceans, is the smallest. It lies at the top of the world and much of it remains frozen throughout the year. It is much shallower than any of the other oceans, although it is comfortably deep enough for submarines which often travel below the ice-cap.

COMPREHENSION

A Write a sentence to answer each question.

1 Is there water on Mars?

2 Which two chemicals together make water?

3 What would happen to the water in the oceans if the Earth moved closer to the sun?

4 What does sea water contain that is not found in rainwater?

B Without looking back at the passage or Fact File, choose the correct word in *italics* to complete these sentences. Write them out.

1. *Earth/Mars/Venus* is the only planet with water.
2. The largest ocean is the *Atlantic/Pacific/Arctic*.
3. From its base on the sea-bed to its summit, Mauna Kea is *123 metres/1023 metres/10,203 metres.*
4. The lost city of Atlantis is said to have been on an island in the *Indian/Atlantic/Pacific* Ocean.
5. The Indian Ocean is roughly *half the size of/the same size as/twice the size of* the Pacific Ocean.

C Write a sentence to answer each question.

1. What conditions are essential for water to exist on Earth?
2. List the oceans of the world in order of size.
3. Why do we usually say that Mount Everest, rather than Mauna Kea, is the tallest mountain?
4. How would you react if offered the chance of a submarine voyage in the Arctic Ocean?

VOCABULARY

Dictionary work

appropriate	condense	torrential
depression	civilisation	mysterious

A You probably recognise these words, but defining them precisely can be more difficult. Try it! Find them again in the passage or Fact File, then write a definition for each one, and below it, copy the definition you find in a dictionary.

B 'Submerged' and 'submarine' both begin with 'sub'. What does *sub* mean? Use a dictionary to find ten more words that begin with 'sub'. Write five sentences, each using one of the 'sub' words in a meaningful way.

Metaphors

Metaphors, like **similes**, are expressions that make descriptions more vivid for the reader.

Similes compare two or more things, and start with either ***as*** or ***like***. *Example:* The sea is *like an angry giant*.

Metaphors suggest similarities between very different things, but **don't** use ***as*** or ***like***. *Example:* The sea is an angry giant.

Poets often use **metaphors** to help them because they express meaning vividly in a very few words. James Reeves's description of the sea is especially strong for this reason, making it easy for us to imagine the various characteristics of the sea.

The Sea

The sea is a hungry dog.
Giant and grey.
He rolls on the beach all day.
With his clashing teeth and shaggy jaws

Hour upon hour he gnaws
The rumbling, tumbling stones,
And 'Bones, bones, bones, bones!'
The giant sea-dog moans,
Licking his greasy paws.

And when the night wind roars
And the moon rocks in the stormy cloud,
He bounds to his feet and snuffs and sniffs,
Shaking his wet sides over the cliffs,
And howls and hollos long and loud.

But on quiet days in May or June,
When even the grasses on the dune
Play no more their reedy tune,
With his head between his paws
He lies on the sandy shores,

So quiet, so quiet, he scarcely snores.

James Reeves

A Copy these sentences and say whether each includes a metaphor or simile.

1 He is as deaf as a post.
2 She is as busy as a bee.
3 The sea is a hungry dog.
4 He ran like the wind.
5 That baby is a real live wire.
6 She is a busy bee.
7 The moon was a ghostly galleon.

B Look again at the *metaphors* in **A** and write down what each means.

C Think about three or more things in your classroom or outside that you could describe in vivid terms using metaphors. Write down some examples.

GRAMMAR

Abstract nouns

Most **nouns** refer to objects which you can see and touch.

sea   Atlantic Ocean   whale   ship   submarine

Remember, **abstract nouns** denote qualities, feelings, times or actions which you **can't** see, touch, taste, smell or hear.
Example: A *robber* can be captured by the police, but his crime of *robbery* can only be talked or thought about.

A Complete these sentences by adding an abstract noun that is related to the noun in *italics*. The first is done to help you.

1 An *infant* needs to be protected throughout its *infancy* .
2 The lifeboat *hero* was praised for his ____ .
3 They despised the *coward* for his ____ .
4 The *thief* was prosecuted for ____ .
5 A *child* attends school during its ____ .

Abstract nouns can also be made from adjectives.
Example: The kind man showed his **kindness**.
adjective (kind)   *abstract noun* (kindness)

B List these adjectives and next to each write the abstract noun that can be made from it.

1 angry *anger*   2 happy   3 generous
4 beautiful   5 stupid   6 active

C Write an adjective that is related to each of these abstract nouns.

1 pride *proud*   2 courage   3 humility
4 wisdom   5 jealousy   6 foolishness

CLUE: If your answers are correct, each can be used in this sentence to describe Sarah: *Sarah is a ____ person.*

Abstract nouns can also be made from verbs.

Example: To **free** a trapped dolphin is to give it **freedom**.
verb — *abstract noun*

D Complete these statements with an abstract noun. The first is done to help you.

1 To *deceive* a friend is to practise *deceit*.
2 To *encourage* a child is to give them ____.
3 To *hate* a person is to be guilty of ____.
4 To *grieve* is to experience a feeling of ____.
5 To *please* one's grandparents is to give them ____.

SPELLING

Tips for better spelling: 6

Antonyms are opposites.

Many words have a suffix **able** or **ible**. Unfortunately there is no easy way to remember when to use **able** or when to use **ible**. However, about five times more words end in **able** than end in **ible**, so you're safer using **able**!

This tip will often help too. If the *antonym* of the word starts with **un** it is probable that it is an **able** word, but if the antonym of the word starts with **il**, **in** or **ir**, it is probably an **ible** word.

Examples: *un*eat**able** *ir*resist**ible** *il*leg**ible**

A Write out these sentences.

1 The sharks were invis__ble in the murky waters.
2 A captain is respons__ble for his vessel's safety.
3 The storm did a neglig__ble amount of damage.
4 Do you think it advis__ble to sail today?
5 The engine was unreli__ble.

QUIZ

Spot the vanishing letters

The feminine of *waiter* is *waitress*, **not** waiteress.
We *enter* through an *entrance* **not** an enterance.
Spot which letter must vanish when these words have their suffixes added. Use a dictionary to check your answers.

1 winter + (y) 2 generous + (ity) 3 disaster + (ous)
4 exclaim + (ation) 5 humour + (ous) 6 curious + (ity)
7 monster + (ous) 8 tiger + (ess) 9 carpenter + (y)

Jamaica Market

Anansi

Kling Kling

Tiger

Anansi

For a long time Anansi tried to catch Kling Kling. They were friends no longer. Anansi set traps and hid them in the grass near the berries on which Kling Kling loved to feed. He made the withes from the woods into long, slippery nooses and hid them where Kling Kling liked to walk. But it was no use. Kling Kling was too clever. He saw all the traps and avoided them. Sometimes he would hide in the top of a tree and, without a sound, watch Anansi set a trap; then when it was all done he would suddenly cry out 'Why?' and fly away, leaving Anansi puzzled and angry.

At last Anansi went to his friend Tiger, and said:

'I beg you, Mr Tiger, help me to catch that old Kling Kling bird. He wouldn't pay his fine. He flew away, and I cannot catch him at all.'

'And what will you give me if I help you catch him?' asked Tiger.

'Oh, my sweet Tiger,' said Anansi, 'I will give you a cow.'

'A whole cow?' asked Tiger, who was very greedy and very fond of cow.

'A whole cow, Mr Tiger. I promise,' said Anansi. So Tiger thought and thought for a long time and at last he said:

'I tell you what we will do, Br'er Anansi. I will lie down in the house and pretend to be dead. You must take a bell and walk all round the town calling out at the top of your voice: "The great King Tiger is dead; the great King Tiger is dead." Then all the people will come to the funeral, and you can catch him.'

Now the next day was a great market day. Kling Kling went to the market and bought peas and rice and codfish and plantain and sweet potatoes. While he was buying the sweet potatoes he heard a bell ringing, and he asked the people what it was. 'Ah,' said a stout market-woman, 'the great King Tiger is dead.'

'What! You mean that Tiger, the great Tiger, is dead?' asked Kling Kling.

'Yes,' said the people standing round; 'yes, what she says is true. The great King Tiger is dead.'

'And when did he die?' asked Kling Kling.

'Yesterday just before twelve o'clock.'

'Then,' cried Kling Kling, 'I must hurry away to put on my second-best coat and go to the funeral.' Kling Kling rushed home and put on his second-best two-tailed blue coat and his shoes that were so new that they cried out 'quee-quee' when he walked in them. When he had finished dressing Kling Kling went to Tiger's house. When he got there he saw a great crowd of people outside, and he shook his head and said:

'So the great King Tiger is dead!'

'Yes,' they replied, 'the great King Tiger is dead.'

'When did he die?'

'Yesterday just before twelve,' they replied.

'What killed him? Was it fever? Was it an accident? How did he die?'

'The heat of the weather killed him,' they said.

'And has he laughed at all since he died?' asked Kling Kling.

'No.'

'Then he isn't dead at all,' said Kling Kling. 'Don't you know that a man is not dead until he laughs a big last laugh?'

Tiger was in the nearest room, listening at the window.

When he heard what Kling Kling said he broke out into a great laugh that shook the house, and Kling Kling said, 'Ha-ha, I never yet heard a dead man laugh!' and he flew away. So Tiger never got the cow.

From *Anansi the Spider Man* by Philip M. Sherlock, Jamaica

COMPREHENSION

A Write a sentence to answer each question.

1 Why were Anansi and Kling Kling no longer friends?

2 How did Anansi try to catch the bird?

3 What reward did Anansi offer Tiger if he could catch Kling Kling?

4 How did Kling Kling find out that Tiger was trying to catch him?

Jamaica Market by *Agnes Maxwell-Hall*

Honey, pepper, leaf-green limes,
Pagan fruit whose names are rhymes.
Mangoes, breadfruit, ginger-roots,
Granadillas, bamboo-shoots,
Cho-cho, akees, tangerines,
Lemons, purple Congo-beans,
Sugar, okras, kola-nuts,
Citrons, hairy coconuts,
Fish, tobacco, native hats,
Gold bananas, woven mats,
Plantains, wild-thyme, pallid leeks,
Pigeons with their scarlet beaks,
Oranges and saffron yams,
Baskets, ruby guava jams,
Turtles, goat-skins, cinnamon,
Allspice, conch-shells, golden rum.
Black skins, babel – and the sun
That burns all colours into one.

COMPREHENSION

A Read the poem again before beginning these activities.

1 What do you think the poet means by:

a pagan fruit

b pallid leeks

c babel

If necessary, use a dictionary to help you.

2 The poem is simple, but effective, in helping us to imagine a Jamaican street market. It is mainly a list with each pair of lines rhyming. Write a similar poem, of between four and eight lines, about your local shop or supermarket.

VOCABULARY

Redundant words

Using carefully-chosen adjectives can make our writing more interesting, but we weaken our writing if, too often, we use more than we need.

Example: Kling Kling was too brainy, intelligent and clever to get caught.

In this sentence *brainy, intelligent, clever* all repeat the same idea, so two of the three words are **redundant**.

A Rewrite these sentences without repeating the ideas.

1. Kling Kling was too brainy, intelligent and clever to get caught.
2. The lady in the market was pretty, beautiful and attractive though poor and without much money, so she couldn't afford to buy expensive clothes that cost a lot.
3. The great, huge, enormous crowd thought it was funny, amusing and comical that Tiger should have fallen for such a simple, easy, obvious trick.

PUNCTUATION

Capital letters and commas

A Punctuate this passage, paying particular attention to capital letters and commas.

jamaica an island in the west indies is the third-largest island in the caribbean sea located south of cuba and west of hispaniola jamaica is about 146 miles (235 km) long by 51 miles (82 km) at its widest point and has highlands running from east to west that cover a large proportion of the island the highest part of jamaica is in the blue mountains to the east sugar tropical fruits coffee and cacao are grown in quantity for sale both in jamaica and to other countries

Conversations

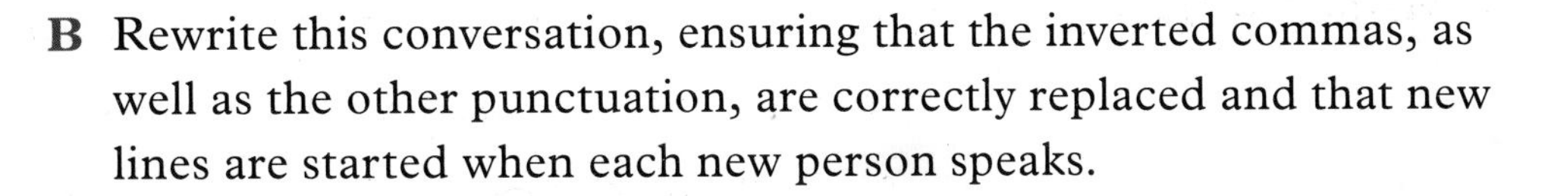

B Rewrite this conversation, ensuring that the inverted commas, as well as the other punctuation, are correctly replaced and that new lines are started when each new person speaks.

Inverted commas are sometimes called 'speech marks'.

did you know that christopher columbus reached jamaica in may 1494 asked the teacher yes i did said the boy my father was telling me about jamaicas history the other day what else did he tell you then enquired the teacher he told me that at that time the island was populated by arawak indians replied the boy but these peoples soon died out and slaves were brought from africa to work in the sugar-cane fields

GRAMMAR

Relative pronouns

Conjunctions are joining words.

Remember, a **pronoun** takes the place of a noun.
Example: Dad said that he would like to visit Jamaica.
He said that he would like to visit Jamaica.

Relative pronouns are special because they do two jobs.

1 They take the place of nouns.
2 They act as conjunctions, and are ***related*** to the noun that is before them in a sentence.
Example: Dad caught the aeroplane.
The aeroplane was flying to Kingston.
Dad caught the aeroplane **which** was flying to Kingston.

The **relative pronouns** are:
who **whom** **whose** **which** **that**

When and **where** are also sometimes used as relative pronouns.

Who is always used for people, **which** is used for things and **that** can be used for either.

A Write these sentences, using *who* or *which* to fill the gaps.

1 This is the picture _____ I want you to give to my grandparents.
2 Tell them it is from their grandson _____ wishes he was coming on the aeroplane.
3 Please thank them for the present _____ they sent for my birthday.
4 In _____ car are you going to the airport?
5 It's a long flight, so don't sit next to anyone _____ snores!

B Rewrite these pairs of sentences as single sentences using *who*, *which* or *that*.

1 I wanted to go with Dad. Dad was going to visit his parents.
2 He took a large box of chocolates. It was a present for my grandparents.
3 My grandparents liked the chocolates. They ate the chocolates straight away.
4 They took Dad to their home. Their home is in Kingston.
5 He was pleased to see the garden. He used to play in it when he was a boy.

SPELLING

Tips for better spelling: 7

To add a suffix to a word that ends in **y** (where the **y** sounds like the *i* in 'tin'), change the **y** to an **i** and add the suffix.
Example: ugl**y** ugl**i**ness

A Add a **ness**, **ment** or **ly** suffix to each of these words, then put it in a sentence. What 'part of speech' is each of your new words in your sentences?

1 merry	2 haughty	3 heavy	4 funny
5 naughty	6 silly	7 pretty	8 nasty

QUIZ

Eights

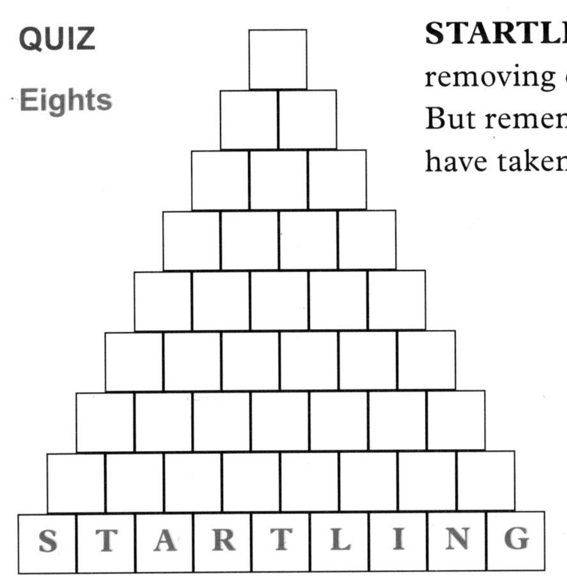

STARTLING can be changed into eight other common words by removing one letter at a time from different places in the word. But remember, you are not allowed to replace a letter once you have taken it out!

THEREIN
has at least eight words hidden in it, without rearranging any of the letters. How many can you find?

UNIT 8

Night

At night you can see the stars twinkling in the vast expanse of outer space. There are billions of stars in the universe, and some of these may have planets like the Earth revolving around them. The universe seems to go on for ever, and no one knows how many stars, planets and satellites it contains.

The sun lies at the centre of our solar system. It is vital to life on Earth. Without its heat and light, nothing could survive on our planet. In the larger world of the universe, however, the sun is just one of millions and millions of quite ordinary stars. It is made of very light hydrogen gas. Nuclear reactions at its centre produce huge amounts of energy which leave the sun as heat and light. The temperature at the centre of the sun is an incredible 15 million degrees Celsius.

Like the sun, the other stars in the galaxy are glowing balls of gas held together by gravity. Reactions in the stars' centres produce heat and light. You can only see the planets and their moons because they reflect the sun's light, but stars shine with their own light.

The stars are so far away that a special unit, called a 'light year', is used to measure the distances between them and the rest of the universe. A light year is the distance that light travels in a year – 9.5 million million kilometres.

A galaxy is an enormous group of stars. Our solar system lies in a galaxy called the Milky Way, which measures about 100,000 light years from side to side. (Compare this with the 8½ minutes which it takes for light to reach Earth from the sun!) There are perhaps 100 thousand million stars in our galaxy, the sun being only one, and there are thousands of millions of galaxies in the universe.

It is difficult to understand how many stars that makes. Small wonder that the night sky is such a truly amazing sight!

Adapted from *What's Out in Space* by Anita Ganeri

COMPREHENSION

A Write a sentence to answer each question.

1 How long does it take for the sun's light to reach Earth?

2 Which is largest, our solar system, the universe or our galaxy?

3 What is the Milky Way, and how big is it?

4 Is the Earth a star or a planet? Explain the difference.

B Write two or three sentences to answer each of these questions.

1 Describe the ideal conditions for observing the stars.

2 If you were offered a trip in a space craft, would you accept? Give reasons for your answer.

3 Explain how the moon can be bathed in sunlight when it is night-time for us.

VOCABULARY

Words change

Our universe is constantly changing, with new stars being created, gradually changing and eventually exploding and dying. Our planet Earth was probably just a ball of gas when it was first created, but it has evolved to a point where it can now support life.

Language too is changing all the time, with new words being needed and existing words being changed or dropped from everyday use altogether. If you were able to listen to people speaking who lived several hundred years ago you would find it difficult to understand them. Many words would be completely different, but some would seem familiar, as hundreds of today's commonly-used words have their roots in Old English (OE).

Example: **hamlet** = a small village [from OE *ham*, home]

A Supply the missing words from these dictionary entries. You have a clue from the Old English (OE) word from which each of the modern English words has come. The first is done to help you.

1 *drift* to move with the wind or tide [OE *drifan*, to drive]

2 ____ not often [OE *seldan*, rare]

3 ____ sour, sharp or painful [OE *biter*, to bite]

4 ____ a container [OE *buc*, a pitcher]

5 ____ to be consumed by worry [OE *fretan*, to eat away]

GRAMMAR

Verbs
Active and passive

Remember, verbs are **active** when the subject of the sentence *does* the action.

Example: Stars **lit** the sky.
subject active verb

Verbs are **passive** when the subject of the sentence has the action *done to it.*

Example: The sky **was lit** by stars.
subject passive verb

A Rewrite these sentences with the verb changed from active to passive, so that the subject has the action done to it. The first is done to help you.

1 The sun lights up the Earth.
The Earth is lit by the sun.

2 Huge meteorites hit Jupiter in 1994.

3 The scientists photographed the eclipse of the sun.

4 The 'Night Sky' television programme told us about the Milky Way.

A partial eclipse of the sun

B Now rewrite these sentences with the verbs changed from passive to active.

1 My eyes were blinded with stars.

2 The girls were fascinated by the vastness of the universe.

3 The moon was eclipsed by the Earth.

4 The astronauts were amazed by the sheer beauty of the Earth.

SPELLING

Tips for better spelling: 8

To make a noun **plural** we normally **add s**.
Examples: star/stars night/nights

But if the noun ends with **s**, **x**, **ch** or **sh** we add **es**.
Examples: bu**s**/buses fo**x**/foxes
chur**ch**/churches bu**sh**/bushes

If a noun ends in **y**, we usually change **y** to **i** and add **es**.
Example: stor**y**/stories

But if the letter before the **y** is a ***vowel***, simply **add s**.
Example: d**a**y/days

A Write the plural of each of these words.

1 poet 2 star 3 rush 4 activity
5 curry 6 alley 7 pony 8 satellite
9 difficulty 10 box 11 valley 12 quay
13 company 14 grass 15 torch 16 ceremony
17 sound 18 father 19 moon 20 country

QUIZ

Lost planets

Each of these letter strings contains two words: one is a planet (for example *Mars*) and the other is a word from the passage (for example *stars*). The letters are in their correct order, but are mixed together.
Example: smatarrss *Answer: Mars/stars*

(Notice that the capital letters are omitted – to make it more difficult!)

Now try these:

1 gmaleracxuryy 2 juhpydirtogeenr 3 nceelpstiuunse
4 uunriavenruses 5 snautclueranr 6 savteellnituess

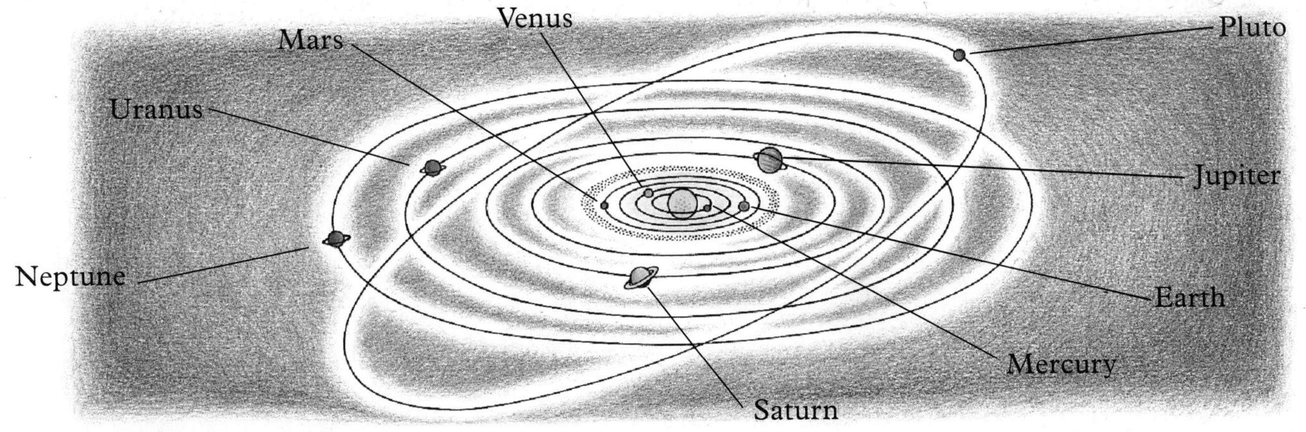

Rainforests – what's the fuss about?

Farming in the rainforest

Rainforest, Brazil

Life can be difficult for those who live in the countries that have rainforests. Some people have insufficient food to eat, and the forest areas are where they can grow food and earn a living to enable them to buy essentials for their survival. The largest rainforest, in the basin of the River Amazon which is largely in Brazil, is still mainly jungle, although thousands of square miles have been cleared in recent years. In the rest of the world, many of the rainforests have been almost completely destroyed.

Every year jungle trees are felled for hardwood timber, which is valued in furniture making, and to make room for mining, growing crops or raising cattle. What is not always realised, however, is that once the trees are cut down and the jungle environment destroyed, the soil is very easily washed away into the great rivers by the torrential rains. What soil is left soon loses its goodness and cannot support agriculture.

Using the forests is not, as some people in the richer countries have suggested, wrong. The local peoples in the poorer countries need to farm, and have a right to; and to earn money from their natural resources, which helps to pay for such important things as new roads and hospitals. What they don't always realise, though, is that countries far away (including Britain!) are polluting the atmosphere with chemicals. The rainforests not only help to remove many of these dangerous gases from the atmosphere, but also make much of the oxygen which we breathe.

Reforestation, Brazil

Rainforest ranch, Amazon

Scientists are also now beginning to recognise that the jungles of the world, with their great natural wealth, contain many plants from which natural medicines can be developed to cure many diseases, possibly even cancer.

For all of these reasons it is extremely important that the remaining forest areas are saved – but how?

Governments can pass laws to protect their own jungles. Companies can create jobs so that fewer people have to use and work in the rainforests. Countries can stop importing the irreplaceable hardwoods from jungle trees.

Scientists are seeking ways to farm in the forests without destroying the soil. In Brazil, for example, people are being encouraged to plant thin strips of land with crops, between which strips of rainforest are left standing. This greatly helps to prevent the soil from being eroded.

More than half the plants and creatures which live in rainforests don't live anywhere else. It is an important responsibility for our generation to ensure that they continue to survive for future generations.

COMPREHENSION

A State whether each of these sentences is 'true' or 'false'.

1. Rainforests occur everywhere that it rains.
2. The largest area of rainforest is in the area of the Amazon River.
3. Throughout the world the area covered by rainforests is gradually increasing.
4. Rainforests are sometimes cleared to enable local people to grow crops, or for mining to take place.
5. When jungle areas are cleared, soils are more easily washed away by the torrential rain.
6. The Amazon flows mainly through Argentina.

B Write several sentences to answer each question.

1. Imagine that you are a Brazilian farmer. You are visited by a European politician who is trying to persuade you to conserve the rainforests. What would you say to her?
2. What actions might people who live in Europe take to help ensure that the rainforests are not destroyed as quickly as they have been in the past?

Growing black pepper, Brazil

VOCABULARY

Prefixes

Prefixes extend or change the meanings of words, and so are important in the English language.

Remembering the main prefixes can help to improve your spelling.

Here is a table of frequently used prefixes with some of their meanings. Unfortunately, some prefixes have several meanings!

If a word has a prefix – just add it!

Prefix	Meaning	Examples
anti	against	anticlockwise
bi	two	bicycle
dis	away, off	dismount
ex	out of	export
fore	previous	foresee
im/in	into	import
im/in	not	impossible, incapable
inter	between	international
ir	not	irreplaceable
mis	wrong	misbehave
non	not	nonsense
pre	before	prefix
re	again	replay
sub	under	subway
trans	across	transatlantic
un	not	unsafe

A 1 Ask your teacher for a photocopy of this table, or copy it neatly into your book. Add at least two other examples for each of the prefixes.

2 Compose a sentence with as many words as possible that have prefixes.

GRAMMAR

Types of clause

Remember: **main** clauses make sense by themselves.
Subordinate clauses help the main clause but do not make sense without the main clause.

Example: The soil gets washed away / when it is left bare.
main clause — *subordinate clause*

The soil gets washed away	makes sense by itself. It is therefore a **main** clause.
when it is left bare	does *not* make sense without the main clause. It is therefore a **subordinate** clause.

Subordinate clauses are often joined to main clauses by conjunctions or pronouns such as:

although before so until (*conjunctions*)
who whose which that when where (*pronouns*)

A Use different colours to underline the main and the subordinate clauses in these sentences.

1. Life can be difficult for poor people who live in the rainforests.
2. Companies can build factories and create jobs so that fewer people have to use the rainforests.
3. It is important that we solve this problem before all the jungles are destroyed.

B Add a subordinate clause that begins with the word in brackets so as to create an interesting sentence.

1. Scientists are seeking new ways to farm (so) ____ .
2. There was not a serious problem (until) ____ .
3. The Amazon Basin has the largest rainforest in the world, (which) ____ .

SPELLING

Fifteen tricky words

Here are fifteen words which occur in the passage in some form, and which can cause spelling problems.

sufficient	essential	survive	destroy
irreplaceable	torrential	pollute	
resources	atmosphere	medicine	diseases
environment	generation	scientist	government

A 1 Make a list of the words, putting them in alphabetical order.

2 Give a synonym and an antonym for the seven words which are in the upper part of the box.

QUIZ

What's missing?

Here is a short paragraph. All the spaces, capital letters, apostrophes and full stops have been taken out. Write it out properly.

britainsnaturalforestsarenowprotectedandarebeingextendedlar
geareasinuplandregionshavebeenplantedwithconifertreestohelpm
eetourtimberneedsmanypeoplearguethattheseareunnaturalandspo
ilthelandscapewhatdoyouthink

Forest in Glen Hurich, Scotland

Machines and people

The Computer's First Christmas Card

jollymerry
hollyberry
jollyberry
merryholly
happyjolly
jollyjelly
jellybelly
bellymerry
hollyheppy
jollyMolly
marryJerry
merryHarry
hoppyBarry
heppyJarry
boppyheppy
berryjorry
jorryjolly
moppyjelly
Mollymerry
Jerryjolly
bellyboppy
jorryjoppy
hollymoppy
Barrymerry
Jarryhappy
happyboppy
boppyjolly
jollymerry
merrymerry
merrymerry
merryChris
annerryasa
Chrismerry
asMERRYCHR
YSANTHEMUM

Edwin Morgan

Don't

Don't put toffee in my coffee
don't pour gravy on the baby
don't put beer in his ear
and don't stick your toes up his nose
don't put the confetti on the spaghetti
and don't squash peas on your knees

don't put ants in your pants
don't put mustard in the custard
don't chuck jelly at the telly
and don't throw fruit at the computer
don't throw fruit at the computer
don't what?
don't throw fruit at the computer
don't what?
don't throw fruit at the computer

Michael Rosen

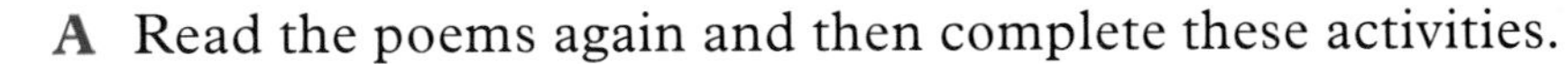

COMPREHENSION

A Read the poems again and then complete these activities.

1 Make a list of the pairs of rhyming words in Michael Rosen's poem *Don't*.

2 a List the words about Christmas which are buried in *The Computer's First Christmas Card*. These will get you started: *jolly* *merry*

b Now make a list of the same poem's nonsense words.

B Try writing a computer poem of your own similar to either of the poems on the opposite page. Use one of these titles, or choose your own: I like . . .
The people who operate me.

VOCABULARY

Improving your writing

Read this extract quietly to yourself. It is from Brian Stone's poem, *The Smiths*.

> Swarthy smoke-blackened smiths, smudged with soot,
> Drive me to death with the din of their banging.
> Men never knew such a noise at night!
> Such clattering and clanging, such clamour of scoundrels!
> Crabbed and crooked, they cry, "Coal! Coal!"
> And blow with their bellows till their brains burst.

In his poem, Brian Stone uses several of the devices we have been practising, to add emphasis and colour to his writing.

Alliteration The same letter sounds are repeated in words that are close together.
Example: **C**rabbed and **c**rooked, they **c**ry, "**C**oal! **C**oal!"

A 1 Copy out two other lines from the poem that use alliteration.

2 Use alliteration in a sentence about a bulldozer.

Onomatopoeia Some words or phrases sound like the noise which they describe. This is onomatopoeia.
Example: Such **clattering** and **clanging**

B Copy this list of machines, and next to each, write as many suitable onomatopoeic words as you can.

1 pneumatic road drill
2 heavy crane
3 chainsaw
4 fruit machine

Word repetition Occasional repetition of the same word.
Example: **Such** clattering and clanging, **such** clamour of scoundrels!

C Write a short sentence for each of these phrases.

1 slower and slower
2 on and on
3 up and up
4 through and through

Synonyms *Examples:* din noise clamour

D Write several synonyms for each of these words that might be used when writing about machines.

1 smell
2 large
3 fast
4 heavy

Idioms Short phrases or sentences that don't mean literally what they say, are idioms. *Example:* Drive me to death

E What is meant by each of these idioms?

1 I thought my head would burst.
2 Let's put our heads together.
3 He was caught red-handed.

PUNCTUATION

Direct speech

A Much of the punctuation is missing from the brief conversation at the top of the next page. Write it again, paying particular attention to the inverted commas, commas, and where new lines should begin.

Hi Jane shouted Bob that's quite some machine youre driving there. She certainly is a real beauty and strong too Jane replied but really easy to handle. All the controls are power-assisted in fact its more like flying a plane than driving an earth-mover. Can i have a go he asked. Sorry old mate it's more than my jobs worth to let anyone near her, Jane shouted secretly pleased that she alone had been trusted to drive the new machine.

SPELLING

Tips for better spelling: 9

To make the plurals of nouns that end in **f** or **fe**, we usually change the **f** or **fe** to **v**, and add **es**.
Examples: wolf, wol**ves** wife, wi**ves**

Beware! There are several important exceptions.

A Write the plural of each of these words that end with **f** or **fe**. Some follow the rule, but some don't.

1. A person who steals
2. Young of a cow
3. Grows on a tree
4. Used to eat with
5. For blowing your nose on
6. Large, wild dog
7. For keeping your neck warm
8. Bread
9. Head of a tribe
10. Two quarters

QUIZ

Get it right

We normally write using 'Standard English'. In each of these sentences one word is wrong. Copy the sentences correctly, and underline the words you have needed to alter.

1. The bulldozer and the digger was both working flat out.
2. Mine is the best of the two computers.
3. Dad said he'd take Wes and I in his new lorry.
4. We was both very excited.
5. Whose left the printer on?
6. May I lend your tools please?

Check-up 2

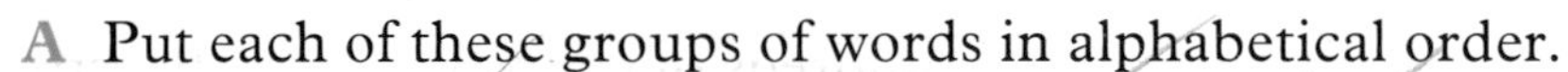

VOCABULARY

A Put each of these groups of words in alphabetical order.

1 hope honour hopeful hoping have hair hare

2 friend free French France freely fresh

3 maths Manchester man matter material mouse

B Copy these sentences, omitting the **redundant words**.

1 London is a huge big city.

2 We were pleased and happy to have the chance of the opportunity to go on the fascinating, interesting visit.

3 We visited a lot of many interesting sites worth seeing.

C Give at least one meaning for each of these **prefixes**.

1 mis 2 anti 3 un 4 pre 5 sub

PUNCTUATION

A Rewrite this passage, adding all the capital letters and punctuation marks which have been omitted, and beginning new lines where necessary.

where are we going first jim asked mr jake his teacher well came the reply that all depends on the traffic if we get to central london before about eleven oclock we can go to the mall and watch the welsh guards changing the guard at buckingham palace what will we do if we miss that asked jim never short of questions we shall go straight to see nelsons column in trafalgar square retorted the irritated teacher who was more interested in studying the street map than answering a barrage of questions from young jim

GRAMMAR

A Write an **abstract noun** related to each of these adjectives.

1 curious 2 happy 3 jealous 4 generous 5 weak

B Copy these sentences, choosing **who** or **which** to fill the gaps.

1 This is a worksheet ____ I want you to complete.

2 Find a guide ____ can help you answer the questions.

3 Here is your ticket, ____ you mustn't lose.

4 There will be a prize for the person ____ completes the work most thoroughly.

C Rewrite these sentences with the verb changed from **active** to **passive**.

1 The bright city lights lit up the sky.

2 Hundreds of people crowded the streets.

3 Our coach driver took us to Oxford Street.

D Underline the **main clause** in each of these sentences.

1 We all settled back in our seats as the coach began the long drive home.

2 The coach stopped at the services on the motorway so that we could buy some food.

SPELLING

A Each of these words ends with **able** or **ible**. Write the words correctly.

1 imposs____	2 advis____	3 us____
4 approach____	5 neglig____	6 respons____
7 prob____	8 incred____	

B Add the **ly** suffix to each of these words, changing them as necessary.

1 happy 2 nasty 3 merry 4 cheery 5 heavy

C Write the **plural** of each of these words.

1 marsh	2 watch	3 fox	4 bus
5 grass	6 pony	7 roof	8 day
9 difficulty	10 curry	11 wife	12 wolf
13 loaf	14 half	15 thief	

D Find a suitable word, beginning with the letters given, to fill each of the gaps in these sentences.

1 He dropped the antique vase, which was ir____.

2 We were caught without raincoats in the tor____ downpour.

3 The smoke above London is pol____ the atm____ .

UNIT 11

World religions in the UK

Hindu Diwali festival

Ritual greetings, Bristol Mosque

Christian wedding

Jewish Passover meal

Inside a Sikh Gurdwara

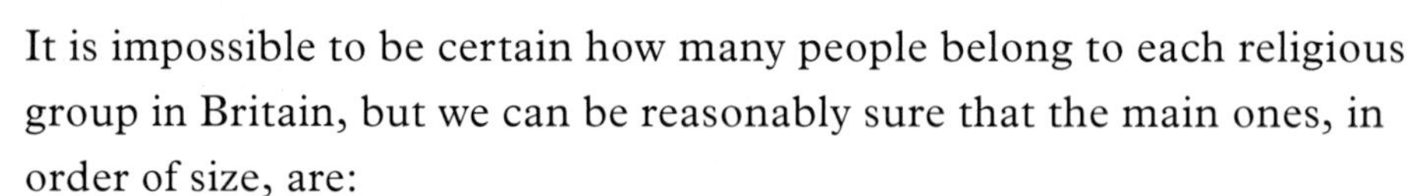

It is impossible to be certain how many people belong to each religious group in Britain, but we can be reasonably sure that the main ones, in order of size, are:

Christians Muslims Sikhs Hindus Jews

Others include Buddhists, Jains, Baha'is, and Parsees or Zoroastrians.

Many people have no religious belief, but most believe they have responsibilities to their fellow human beings and to the planet which we all share. Some of these people call themselves 'humanists'.

Those people who cannot decide whether there is a God call themselves 'agnostic'. Agnostic comes from the Greek for 'not knowing'. 'Atheists' are people who are certain in their minds that there is no God.

Most of the major religious groups are very old, but some were founded more recently.

Calendars can vary in different countries and often date from when a major religious figure was born. In Britain the calendar uses dates from when Jesus Christ was born. The chart below shows when the major religions had their beginnings relative to the Christian calendar. (BC means 'Before Christ'.)

About 2000 BC	Early Hinduism	Hinduism had no single founder
	Early Judaism	Judaism had no single founder, though Abraham lived about 1750 BC
About 600 BC	Zoroaster	The founder of Zoroastrianism
599 BC	Mahavira	The founder of Jainism
563 BC	Buddha	The founder of Buddhism
0	Jesus Christ	The founder of Christianity
570	Muhammad	The 'messenger' of Islam
1469	Guru Nanak	The founder of Sikhism
1817	Baha'ullah	The founder of the Baha'i religion

While the main religions in the UK have different traditions and ways of worship, most share these four principles, which they believe to be important:

helping poorer countries;
protecting the environment;
encouraging people of different racial groups to live together peacefully;
and promoting world peace.

Most of the main religions believe that there is only one God for all people. Different religions are different people's ways of thinking about God, and attempting to understand the meaning of life.

COMPREHENSION

Hindu bride preparing for her wedding

A Finish these sentences and write them out.

1 The five largest religious groups in Britain are ____ .

2 Humanists have no specific religious beliefs but ____ .

3 Agnostics are ____ .

4 Those who are sure that there is no God ____ .

5 Jesus was born ____ Buddha.

B Answer these questions.

1 Which, for you, is the most important of the 'four principles'? Give reasons for your answer.

2 Make a table listing as many religious groups as you can. Next to each, write the name of at least one person who belongs to that group.

Christian	
Muslim	
Hindu	

St. Peter and St. Paul Church, Buckinghamshire

VOCABULARY

Synonyms

The English language is rich in synonyms.
Example: **sure** – certain, positive, satisfied, convinced, confident, assured

A Look at this list of words from the passage and, without referring to your thesaurus, write as many synonyms as you can (which may be one word or a short phrase) for each.

1 belief 2 major 3 old 4 environment
5 impossible 6 god 7 group 8 important

B Now check what you have written by referring to a thesaurus, adding any additional words which are listed.

Eponyms

Several of the names of major religions are **eponyms**. An eponym is a word or title which is based on a person's name.
Example: **Buddhism** is named after Buddha.

A Find at least two other religious groups whose names are eponyms.

Several other words we use quite frequently are **eponyms**.
Example: **Wellingtons**, the long rubber boots, are named after the first Duke of Wellington.

B Choose five of these words to research, using dictionaries, an encyclopedia and any other suitable reference books. Find all you can about the origin of the words.

guillotine
Pennsylvania
volt
pasteurise
saxophone
macintosh
cardigan
sandwich
biro
quisling
shrapnel
Braille

Boy reading Braille

PUNCTUATION

Colons

The main function of a **colon** (:) is to introduce a list.

Example: These are the most popular religious groups in Britain: Christians, Muslims, Sikhs, Hindus and Jews.

A Copy these sentences, adding **colons** and commas where necessary.

1 There are important religious festivals on the following dates January 6th February 12th April 3rd May 16th and June 10th.

2 The following have been selected to sing solos next week Ben William Claire Annie Sunil and Roy.

3 I have chosen these hymns 15 243 78 46 and 55.

GRAMMAR

Using auxiliary verbs

Auxiliary verbs are words like **have, has, had, can, could**.

Auxiliary verbs (helping verbs) are useful in telling us when to use the different forms of some verbs.

Example: Never use an **auxiliary verb** with *came*.
Normally use an **auxiliary verb** with *come*.

We *came* to the festival.
We **have** *come* to the festival.

We *never* use an auxiliary verb with:
came, rang, drank, began, took, ran, ate

We *normally* need an auxiliary verb with:
come, rung, drunk, begun, taken, run, eaten

A Copy these sentences, selecting the correct verbs. Underline the auxiliary verbs when they appear.

1. I rang/rung the church bell this morning.
2. I had not rang/rung it for the last three months.
3. The service began/begun at 9.30 a.m.
4. It had began/begun before I had finished ringing!
5. The verger come/came in and took/taken the bell-rope from me.
6. If I had took/taken my watch I wouldn't have made the mistake.
7. I run/ran home feeling very upset.
8. I felt better after I had drank/drunk a cup of tea and ate/eaten a biscuit.
9. The vicar came/come to our house and told me not to worry.

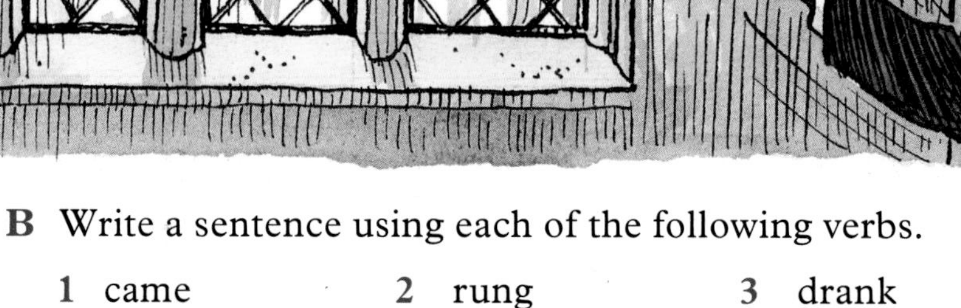

B Write a sentence using each of the following verbs.

1 came	2 rung	3 drank
4 begun	5 took	6 eaten

SPELLING

Tips for better spelling: 10

To make plurals of most nouns that end in **o** we add **es**.
Example: one tomat**o** two tomat**oes**

Be careful! These are some important exceptions:
photos hippos radios rhinos pianos

Music words and words ending in **oo** are also exceptions, and we just add **s** to make them plural.
Example: one cuck**oo** two cuck**oos**

Two of these can be spelt both ways.

A Write the plural of each of these words.

1 soprano	**2** hero	**3** volcano	**4** potato
5 photo	**6** motto	**7** cuckoo	**8** piano
9 radio	**10** cockatoo	**11** cello	**12** echo

QUIZ

Religious research

Copy and complete this table by asking friends or by researching in your library. Can you think of more religious groups to add to the list?

Religious group	**Most important day of week**	**Place of worship**	**Founder or important prophet**	**Building of special significance**
Baha'is				
Buddhists				
Christians				
Hindus				
Jains				
Jews				
Muslims				
Rastafarians				
Sikhs				

UNIT 12

The great dinosaur mystery

For over 150 million years the Earth was dominated by some of the most extraordinary creatures that ever lived – the great reptiles, popularly known as the dinosaurs. The name 'dinosaur', first introduced by zoologist Richard Owen, is Greek for 'terrible lizard', though dinosaurs were not true lizards. Whilst most dinosaurs were vegetarians, the few flesh-eaters were indeed terrible. So why, from having been the lords of the Earth 65 million years ago, did the dinosaurs suddenly die out, leaving the world to the smaller mammals?

Scientists have made several attempts to resolve the riddle. Did the climate change? Did certain smaller animals take to eating the dinosaurs' eggs? Did a nearby exploding star shower the Earth with deadly X-rays? Some doubted an answer would ever be found.

Then, about twenty years ago, some very rare material, iridium, was found – in rocks about 65 million years old. Where did it come from, and could it be significant that it first appeared just when the dinosaurs died out?

Meteor crater, Arizona, USA

Scientists now believe that the most likely origin of the iridium was outer space, and that it probably arrived as part of one or more large meteorites which collided with Earth. The craters caused by these meteorites have now been worn away, but some are more recent, such as those in the pictures, and can still be seen today.

But how could something striking the Earth 65 million years ago have killed all the dinosaurs?

The theory is that if the object had been big enough it could have caused such a devastating impact that it would have thrown enormous amounts of rock and dust high into the atmosphere. The dust would have spread round the world, cutting out much of the sunlight. For months or even years there would have been little light and heat. It would have been rather like a permanently frosty night. Plants would have died and then the animals that lived on the plants would have starved. Small animals might have been able to survive by nibbling bark or seeds, or even the frozen bodies of larger animals. But by the time the skies had cleared and the warmth and light from the sun shone through again, it would have been too late for the dinosaurs.

Meteor crater, Arizona, USA

COMPREHENSION

A Write a sentence or sentences to answer each question.

1 What does 'dinosaur' mean?

2 What is a vegetarian?

3 Why are dinosaurs described as 'lords of the Earth'?

4 Give the main possibilities to explain why dinosaurs became extinct.

Synonyms are words with similar meanings.

B 1 Copy these words from the passage, and next to each write a synonym.

extraordinary	devastating
resolve	significant
origin	collided

2 Of the theories offered for the death of the dinosaurs, which do you think most likely to be true? Give your reasons, and explain why you are less sure about the others.

VOCABULARY

Using a thesaurus

730

term

time
period
spell
season
duration
cycle
termly
terminal
[see 472, 747]

731

terrible

awful
shocking
frightful
horrible
gruesome
horrendous
terribly
[see 44, 587]

732

terrific (1)

ter
ter
[see

73

terri

marv
fanta
excep
wond
treme
sensa
[see

73

terr

frigh
shoc
scar
terr
hor
petr
terri
terri
[see

When wishing to write about dramatic situations or events, it can sometimes be difficult to find the words to best express the tension or emotions, or describe the scene. This is when a **thesaurus** can be helpful.

Example: **terrible**
awful
shocking
frightful
horrible
gruesome
horrendous
terribly

A List the words in your thesaurus that appear under these headings. Underline the ones you might select if you were writing an adventure story called 'The Return of the Dinosaurs' for your school magazine.

1 damage	2 cry	3 afraid
4 grab	5 harm	6 terrible
7 brave	8 prevent	9 sad

Improving sentences

When checking sentences that we have written, we should think whether to **change** some of the words to **improve** them.

Example: The truck skidded **a bit** and **got** stuck.
The truck skidded **uncontrollably** and **became** stuck.

Words for which we can usually find a better alternative include:
nice **lot** **bit** **got**

Tyrannosaurus

A Rewrite these sentences to avoid using *nice*, *lot*, *bit* and *got*.

1. I got a bit of a shock.
2. A lot of us were looking at the nice exhibits.
3. They looked nice, though there were a lot of them.
4. I, and a lot of my friends, got a bit tired.
5. One of the dinosaurs had got a nice face.
6. A lot of us were drawing it.
7. We are sure it gave us a bit of a smile.
8. Imagine the shock we got!
9. Dad said it was a nice story – but he didn't believe a bit of it!

Dinosaur Park

GRAMMAR

Expanding sentences

Remember, phrases don't have a proper verb – clauses do!

As well as **changing** sentences to **improve** them, they can be **expanded** to make them more interesting or clearer by adding **words, phrases** or **clauses**.

Example: The dinosaur ate the leaves.
The **enormous** dinosaur **extended its giraffe-like neck and contentedly** ate the **succulent green** leaves.

When looking at a sentence that you have written, ask yourself, 'Do I need to add more detail to answer the questions:

What kind? To what degree? When? How?
Which? Where? How often? How much? How many?'

A Expand each of these sentences to answer the questions shown in the brackets.

1. A dinosaur was sleeping. (What kind? Where? How?)
2. It opened its eyes. (Why? How?)
3. It saw another dinosaur coming. (Where? What kind? How?)
4. It stood up. (How? Why?)
5. There was a fight. (When? What kind?)
6. The dinosaur went back to sleep. (When? Where? To what degree?)

B Think carefully how each of these ten sentences might be expanded by adding suitable words, phrases and clauses where appropriate. Write them out.

1. The scientists went exploring for dinosaur skeletons.
2. Their vehicle headed through the desert.
3. They found a crater.
4. It was deep.
5. The truck became stuck.

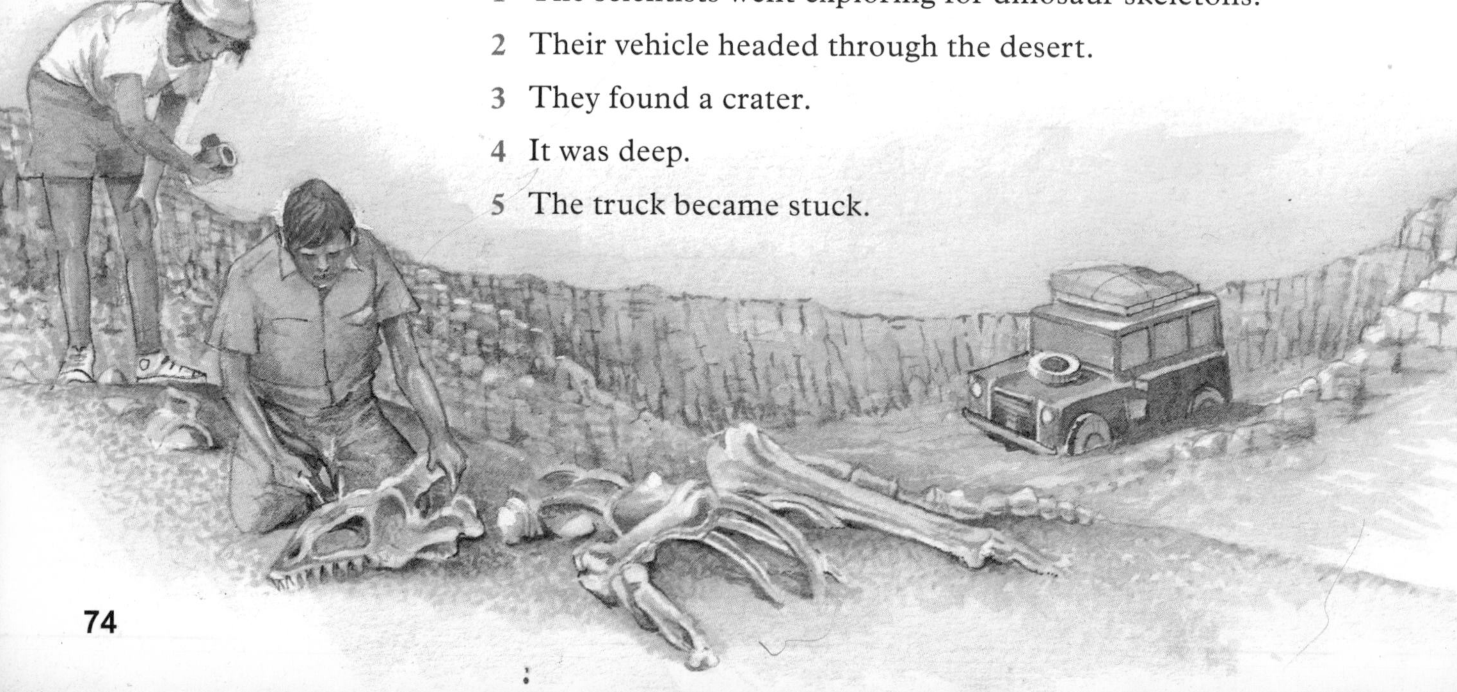

6 Darkness fell and it became cold.

7 Wild animals were nearby.

8 In the morning they saw a helicopter.

9 It spotted them.

10 It landed and helped them.

SPELLING

Thirty tricky words

Look
Cover
Remember
Write
Check

Here are 30 words that frequently cause spelling difficulties. Use your dictionary to complete them correctly.

1	reco_nise	2	mini_ture	3	sep_rate
4	beca_se	5	lib_ary	6	shep__rd
7	parl__ment	8	con_cious	9	cu_board
10	enco_rage	11	happ_ness	12	burgl_r
13	ex_ellent	14	justi_e	15	jew__
16	nei__bour	17	vill__n	18	rec__ve
19	cus_ion	20	admi__ion	21	addi_ion
22	grud_e	23	presen_e	24	miser_ble
25	photogra__	26	c_oir	27	colum_
28	obstin_te	29	a_kward	30	obst_cle

QUIZ

Odd one out

Which is the odd one out in each of these groups? Give the reason for your answer. You may need to do some research in your library.

1 diplodocus melanosaurus tyrannosaurus apatosaurus

2 brachiosaurus compsognathus coelophysis protoceratops

3 megalosaurus stegosaurus allosaurus parasaurolophus

UNIT 13

Dragons – fact or fiction?

Myths and legends involving dragons are common throughout the world, being handed down from generation to generation. The red dragon is to this day one of the main emblems of Wales, and the legend of England's patron saint, St George, involves a dragon which he killed in order to save the life of a princess.

Most dragons are portrayed as having a reptilian body and wings or the head and forelegs of a lion or bird of prey. Often they breathe fire, and many are associated with water. Whilst most dragons are portrayed as evil creatures, this has not always been the case in China, where many were depicted in a good light and taken as the Emperors' symbol. Indeed, a dragon was the main emblem on the Chinese flag in the period of the Ch'ing dynasty in the nineteenth century.

The Dragon of Death

In a faraway, faraway forest
lies a treasure of infinite worth,
but guarding it closely forever
looms a being as old as the earth.

Its body is big as a boulder
and armoured with shimmering scales,
even the mountaintops tremble
when it thrashes its seven great tails.

Its eyes tell a story of terror,
they gleam with an angry red flame
as it timelessly watches its riches,
and the dragon of death is its name.

Its teeth are far sharper than daggers,
they can tear hardest metal to shreds.
It has seven mouths filled with these weapons,
for its neck swells to seven great heads.

Each head is as fierce as the other,
Each head breathes a fiery breath,
and any it touches must perish,
set ablaze by the dragon of death.

All who have foolishly stumbled
on the dragon of death's golden cache
remain evermore in that forest,
nothing left of their bodies but ash.

Jack Prelutsky

With so many myths and legends involving dragons, one is left wondering whether such creatures once actually existed – or have they all been figments of the imagination of storytellers and poets down the ages?

Just to the east of the Indonesian island of Java lies a group of smaller islands which includes Komodo, Rintja, Flores and Padar. The islands are not well known in themselves, but they are famous to zoologists as being the home of a remarkable animal, the largest of all known lizards. These are the great reptiles scientists call *Varanus komodoensis*, but their popular name is 'Komodo dragon', which is appropriate because they are probably the nearest the world has ever come to the far more fantastic creatures of myth and legend.

Komodo dragon, Indonesia

Of course the Komodo dragon does not have the mythical dragon's wings, for of all the reptiles known to have lived on Earth, only the long-vanished pterodactyls have ever flown. Nor does it breathe fire, but it is large (up to three metres long) and powerful. What is more, it fits the 'dragon image' in being a flesh-eater, capable of killing animals as big as a buffalo, which it does by first severing their leg tendons and bringing them crashing to the ground. It will even attack humans if they take too many liberties!

Perhaps not surprisingly, therefore, some people believe that the Komodo dragon may have given the Chinese, Japanese and other Asiatic peoples the basic idea for mythical dragons, from where such ideas spread to the rest of the world.

Adapted from *Did They Exist?* by Anthony Wootton

COMPREHENSION

A Write sentences to answer these questions.

1 Where are Komodo dragons found?

2 To which group of creatures do they belong?

3 Which is the only reptile believed to have had wings?

4 What would be the wisest course of action if you saw a Komodo dragon?

B What do the following words mean as they are used in the passage or the poem?

1 emblem	2 portrayed	3 reptilian	4 depicted
5 dynasty	6 infinite	7 cache	8 severing

VOCABULARY

Puns

A **pun** is a play on words.
Example: "I hope the **dragon** story doesn't ***drag on*** too long," said James.

Some puns involve **homophones** or **homonyms**.
Example: Leila had a toothache. Brian said, "Put your head through the **window** and the ***pain*** will be gone."

A Can you explain these **puns**?

1 The factory workers enjoy dyeing for a living.

2 Headline on a sports page:

MARATHON RUNNER'S GREAT FEAT

3 Another headline:

COACH FIRE – PASSENGERS SAFELY ALIGHT

These puns were seen in a shop:

4 The main route from Ireland

5 Pillars of Ancient Greece

6 Things to adore

GRAMMAR

Abstract nouns and idioms

Remember, most **nouns** are objects which you can see and touch, but **abstract nouns** denote qualities, feelings, times or actions which you can't see, touch, taste, smell or hear.

Examples: hypocrisy cowardice boastfulness submission disgrace boldness selfishness indecision

Idioms are short phrases which mean something quite different from what might be expected.

A Use a dictionary to check the meaning of any of the words in the box above that are unfamiliar to you.

B For each of the **idioms** below, find the abstract noun in the box that is closest to its meaning.

1. Having cold feet
2. Blowing one's own trumpet
3. Being under a cloud
4. Grasping the nettle
5. Throwing in the sponge
6. Feathering one's own nest
7. Blowing hot and cold
8. Shedding crocodile tears

C Select two **suffixes** from the words in the box, and list five other words with the same suffix.

D Write three sentences, each one including one of the **idioms** from **B** so as to demonstrate what it means.

Remember, there are **eight parts of speech**. (Look back to Unit 1 if you need to be reminded.) The four most important are **nouns**, **adjectives** (which describe nouns), **verbs** and **adverbs** (which describe verbs).

Many words can be altered by adding or taking away various **prefixes** and **suffixes**. Some words can have several forms, so that they can become each of these four **parts of speech**.

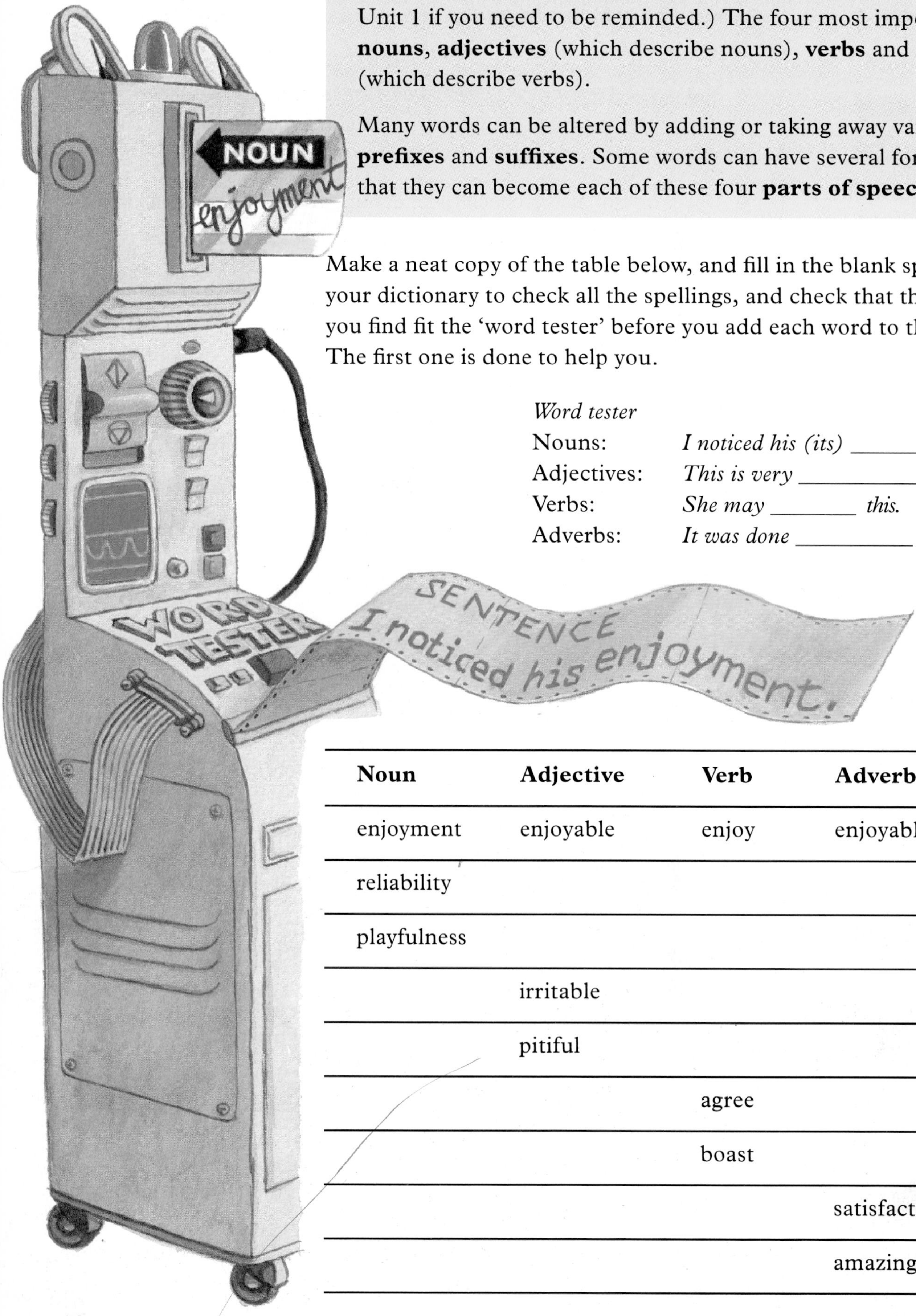

Make a neat copy of the table below, and fill in the blank spaces. Use your dictionary to check all the spellings, and check that the words you find fit the 'word tester' before you add each word to the table. The first one is done to help you.

Word tester

Nouns: *I noticed his (its)* ___________ .

Adjectives: *This is very* ___________ .

Verbs: *She may* _______ *this.*

Adverbs: *It was done* __________ .

NOUN

enjoyment

WORD TESTER

SENTENCE

I noticed his enjoyment.

Noun	Adjective	Verb	Adverb
enjoyment	enjoyable	enjoy	enjoyably
reliability			
playfulness			
	irritable		
	pitiful		
		agree	
		boast	
			satisfactorily
			amazingly

SPELLING

Tips for better spelling: 11

i comes before **e** (when the sound is *ee*)
Examples: piece, relieve, priest

except after **c**
Examples: receive, ceiling, deceive, receipt, conceit

or when the sound is not *ee*
Examples: reign, veil, heir, foreign, sovereign, forfeit

A 1 Write the words in the box below in a long list.

receive field believe wield weigh eight their deceit rein chief shield vein receipt sleight leisure achieve

2 Tick the words in which the **ie** or the **ei** sounds *ee* (as in *bee*).

3 Underline those you have ticked that have an **ei**.

4 What do you notice about the words you have underlined?

5 What do you notice about the words you have not underlined?

QUIZ

'Missing explorers'

Here is a scrap of paper found in a clearing close to a cave where dragons are said to have been spotted. Copy the letter, filling in the missing words, to discover what may have happened to the writer.

If anyone finds this … please be VERY
not to get … in the same
Tell my dear … as I did.
to … that I will … stop trying
from the dragons' … We were
through the dense … when our leader
upon the cave … from which were
coming … noises. The … we heard
was a … and suddenly crashing t…
the undergrowth came … huge, horrifying
…n. I must stop now for I … I can hear
…n.

Cliffs under attack

Where the land and the sea meet, we often find cliffs. Cliffs, like all the land under our feet, may be made from hard, tough rocks such as granite, or from soft, weak material such as clay; some cliffs are made from a mixture of both.

As the waves beat against the bottom of a cliff it is gradually worn away. Water is forced into cracks in the cliffs at wave height, which weakens the rocks, and eventually pieces break away. These get thrown about in the waves, constantly rubbing against each other, eventually breaking down to make smaller rocks, pebbles (or 'shingle') and then fine sand.

If you examine the colour of the sand on a beach you may find it is similar to the colours in the rocks in nearby cliffs. If the beach comes from yellow or red sandstone, it will have yellow sand; if the cliffs are made from coral, the sand is white. If, however, the cliffs are made from volcanic lava rock, the beach sand may be black.

Sometimes there is no beach on a rocky headland. As soon as pieces of rock and sand are washed from the cliff, they are carried away by the powerful waves and currents.

The cliffs in this picture are made of hard rock. They can withstand the mightiest storm. However, the ragged shape shows that the waves are gradually eroding where the rocks are slightly weaker. Where this happens, a cave may be formed. This can gradually become larger until the roof falls in, leaving other interesting rock formations such as 'arches'.

When the upper part of the arch eventually collapses, the remaining pillar of rock is called a 'sea stack'.

COMPREHENSION

A Write a sentence to answer each question.

1. How is the colour of sand on a beach sometimes influenced by rocks in the nearby cliffs?
2. Why are there no beaches in front of some cliffs?
3. How are caves usually formed in sea cliffs?
4. What features may be left after a cave roof collapses?

Onomatopoeic words are 'sound' words.

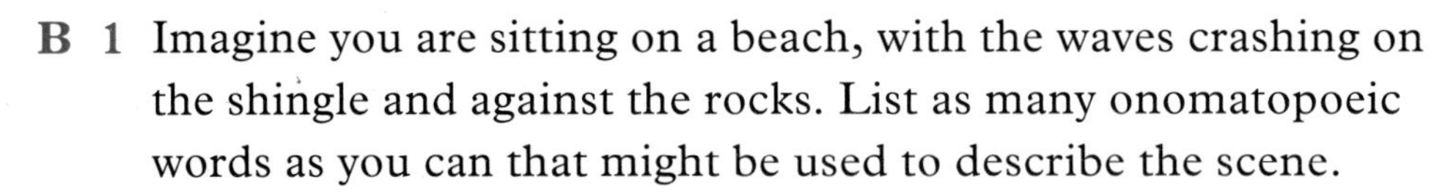

B 1 Imagine you are sitting on a beach, with the waves crashing on the shingle and against the rocks. List as many onomatopoeic words as you can that might be used to describe the scene.

2 Write a number of highly descriptive phrases or sentences about the force and energy of the sea and the waves. Your list might include some similes and metaphors.

VOCABULARY

Definitions

Mare is the Latin word for 'sea'.
The suffix **ine** means 'to do with'.
Therefore **marine** means 'to do with the sea'.

A Work out, or look up, what each of these words means.

1 marina	2 mariner	3 maritime
4 submarine	5 submariner	6 aquamarine

B The word **sea** can be used as part of several compound words. Write one sentence for each of these pairs of words, using them and explaining the difference between them.

1 horse	sea-horse	2 weed	seaweed
3 dog	sea-dog	4 urchin	sea-urchin
5 green	sea-green	6 mile	sea-mile

Word webs

Before writing, it can sometimes be helpful to collect words which may be useful. Making word webs is one way of doing this. For example:

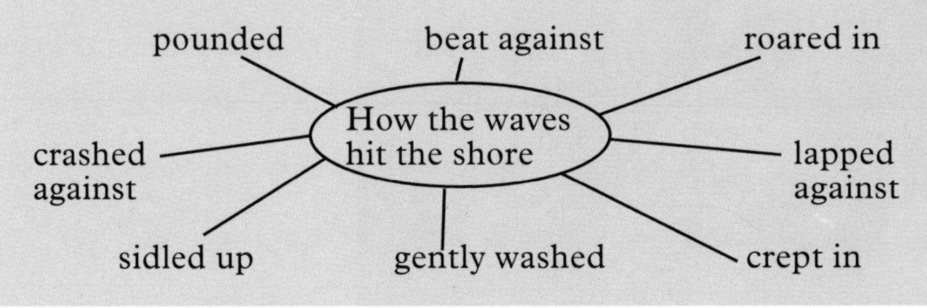

A Make a word web for these.

1 How I feel being trapped on a cliff

2 Textures on a beach

PUNCTUATION

Letters

Here are two letters written by the same person but to different people, and for different reasons. When we are writing letters, the nature and tone of the letters should take account of the impact we want to have on the reader.

A Rewrite this **personal letter** correctly.
Give careful thought to the layout of the letter and to the arrangement of the paragraphs. Clearly, all the capital letters have been omitted, as have all the different forms of punctuation. Start your work at the top of a new page.

23 centre crescent

blaxland

essex

15th july

dear grandma

the holiday is almost here mum and i already have our coach seats booked and we cant wait to see you do you remember last year when we all went for that long walk along the beach towards fishermans cove paddling as we went it was great fun at first but it was really frightening when that large portion of cliff gave way with no warning it was a wonder that no one on the beach was killed we were all very lucky i dont think well go there this year do you well thats enough for now i still have to finish some work in time for school tomorrow please give my love to aunty sue and uncle alan and tell my cousins that im really excited about seeing them again soon i can hardly wait with love freya

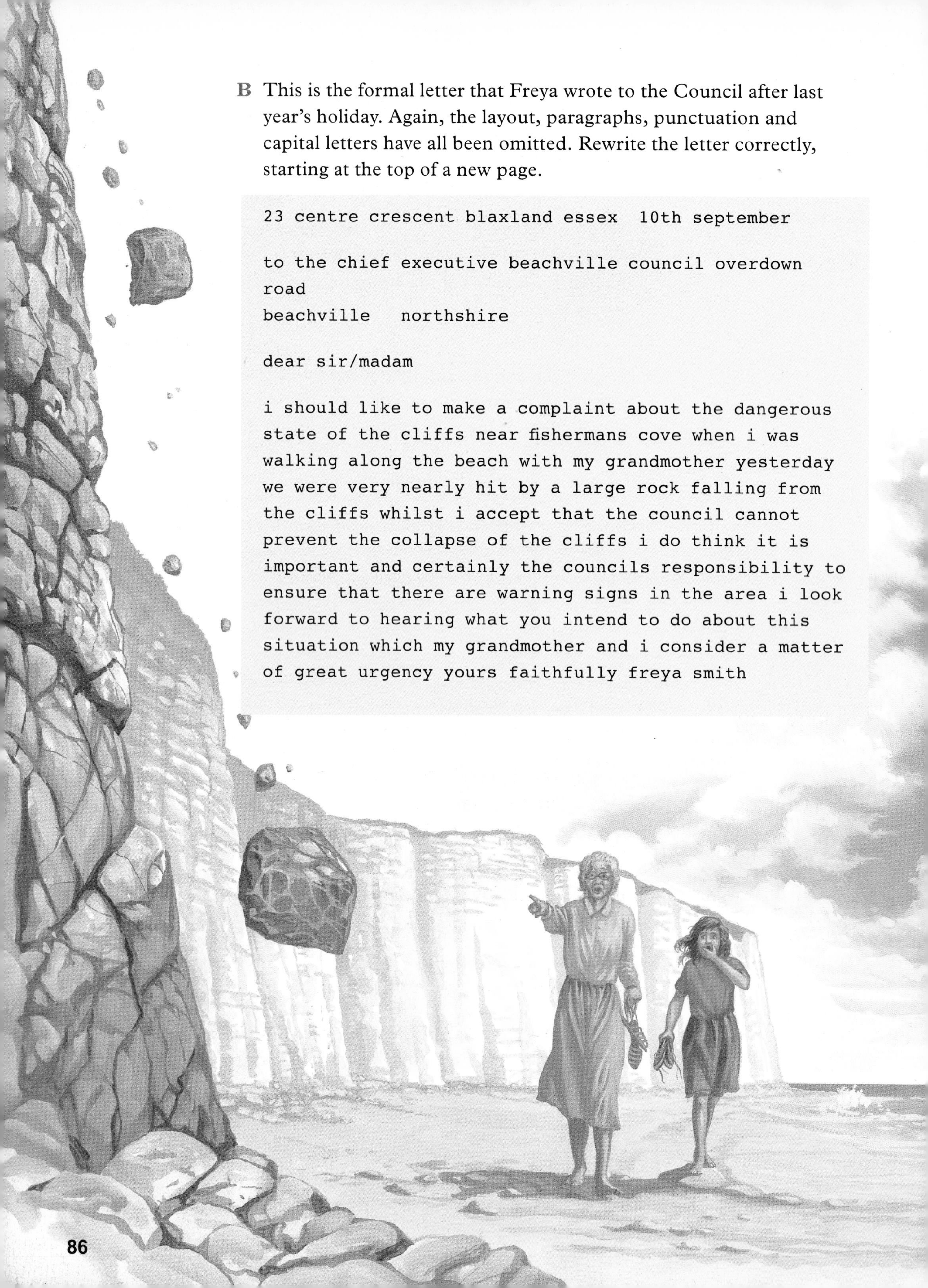

B This is the formal letter that Freya wrote to the Council after last year's holiday. Again, the layout, paragraphs, punctuation and capital letters have all been omitted. Rewrite the letter correctly, starting at the top of a new page.

```
23 centre crescent blaxland essex  10th september

to the chief executive beachville council overdown
road
beachville   northshire

dear sir/madam

i should like to make a complaint about the dangerous
state of the cliffs near fishermans cove when i was
walking along the beach with my grandmother yesterday
we were very nearly hit by a large rock falling from
the cliffs whilst i accept that the council cannot
prevent the collapse of the cliffs i do think it is
important and certainly the councils responsibility to
ensure that there are warning signs in the area i look
forward to hearing what you intend to do about this
situation which my grandmother and i consider a matter
of great urgency yours faithfully freya smith
```

SPELLING

Tips for better spelling: 12

When adding a prefix: **'Just add it!'**
Don't miss out any letters.

Examples: un + sure = unsure
dis + satisfy = dissatisfy

The pair of *s*'s is caused by bringing together the last letter of the prefix with the first letter of the word. Don't be tempted to leave out one of the *s*'s.

A List all the words which have double letters as a result of adding these prefixes.

1	dis +	satisfy	organise	appear
		trust	similar	obey
2	un +	necessary	invited	eventful
		numbered	natural	named
3	over +	reach	turn	rule
		ride	look	run
4	im +	possible	measurable	mortal
		modest	moral	movable

QUIZ

Word pairs

Look at the word in **bold** letters and then select two words from those next to it. One should be an antonym, and the other a synonym, of the word in **bold**.

danger cycling peril excitement safety carelessness
Answer: *peril* (S) *safety* (A)

shout question yell whisper said answer

sudden gradual bang quick loud unusual

climb rock descend high ascend steep

certain improvement sure charming doubtful entirely

protect property fence attack safeguard find

UNIT 15

Lions – the cat facts

Lionesses and cubs

Tiger

Cheetah

The cat family can be divided into 'big cats' and 'small cats', but size is not their only difference.

Big cats	**Small cats**
Examples: lion tiger jaguar	*Examples:* puma cheetah
– roar	– purr
– lie down to feed	– crouch while feeding
– rest with paws and tail stretched out straight	– rest with paws tucked under and tail wrapped around

Karnak, Egypt

Cats have fascinated humans for thousands of years, being first domesticated about 10,000 years ago when wandering tribes first settled into village life. In Egypt about 3000–4000 years ago, all cats were worshipped as sacred animals, but it was lions that were particularly revered.

The most important event in the Egyptian calendar was the annual flooding of the River Nile, bringing as it did the rich, fertile silts. These silts were important for growing the food crops in ancient Egypt, and the lion was believed to control these floods. In many other early civilisations the lion was also linked with the sun. Its golden mane represented the sun's rays and it was a symbol of invincible power and kingship.

Lions have also been used to symbolise bravery in battle, masculinity and watchfulness, as well as courage and generosity. Unfortunately for the lions, however, Assyrian monarchs believed that they could only achieve true kingship by killing a lion – the king of the beasts. They believed this would give them the strength and bravery of the lion.

In the 3rd century BC, the Indian Emperor Ashoka, an early conservationist, erected many pillars inscribed with Buddhist teachings on nature and non-violence. The lion, sacred to the Buddhists, topped many of these columns.

There are now not many Asian lions left, either in India or elsewhere. A small population of about 300 in the north-west of the country is the only surviving group in the wild. Although very similar to their African relative, Asian lions have a long fringe under their belly.

Like most cats, lions' sight has evolved to enable twilight hunting, being especially well equipped to detect slight movements in semi-darkness.

They are also extremely sensitive to sound, being able to hear frequencies much higher than the human ear can detect. None of the cats has a particularly well-developed sense of smell.

Lions, being the supreme animal hunters, and having an aloofness and apparent self-confidence born of invincibility, remain today as always – kings, not only of the cat family, but of all the beasts.

COMPREHENSION

A Choose the most appropriate words from those in *italics* to complete these sentences.

1. 'Big' cats *roar/purr* and *lie down/crouch* to eat.
2. Cats were first kept by humans *one hundred/one thousand/ten thousand* years ago.
3. In early civilisations the *tiger/leopard/lion* was linked with the *moon/sun/Mars* because of its *head/mane/tail.*
4. *Asian/European/African* lions are almost extinct, though a small group remains in the *north-east/south-west/north-west* of India.

B 1 List the words in the passage which describe the characteristics of a lion.

2 Make a table, similar to that on page 88, to compare the main characteristics of domesticated cats and dogs.

3 Choose and list some descriptive words which you might use in a passage to describe a pet or any other animal you know.

VOCABULARY

Collective nouns

Collective nouns are special nouns used for **collections** (or groups) of people, animals or things.

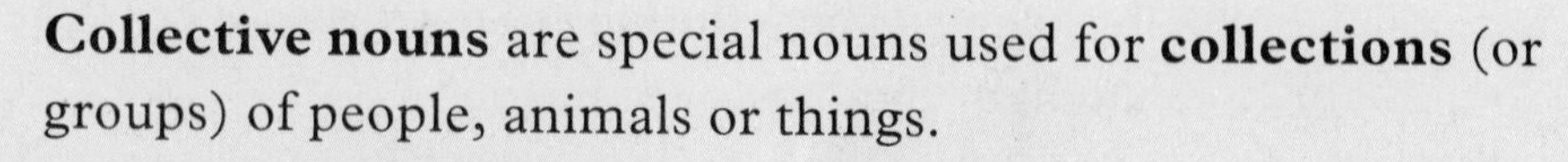

Examples: a **pride** of lions a **litter** of kittens

A All the collective nouns to match the groups in these pictures are listed in the box. Can you sort them?

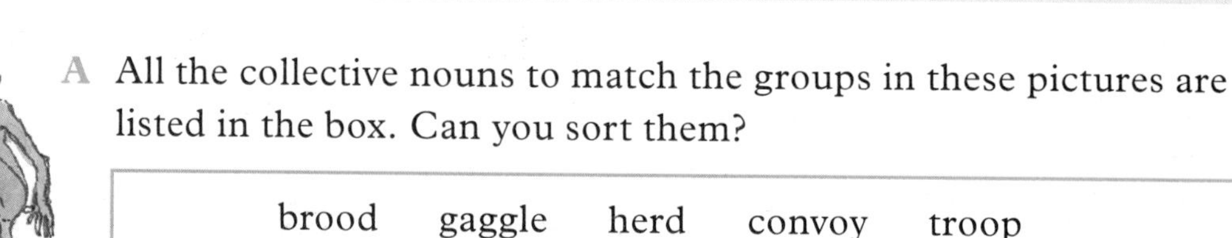

brood gaggle herd convoy troop
pack shoal peal

PUNCTUATION

This section practises all the punctuation marks we have used in *Nelson English*. Can you spot them all? The capital letters have also been omitted, and you will need to think carefully about where to start a new line.

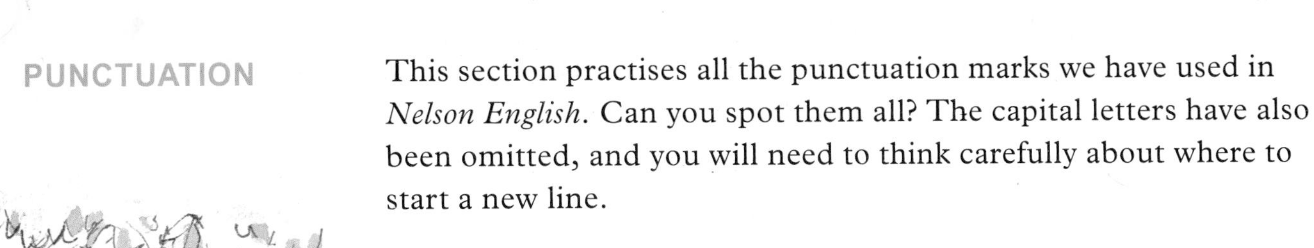

A Rewrite these short passages correctly. They become increasingly difficult, so be careful!

1 some say the lion is the king of the jungle which is strange because lions in africa as well as the few remaining in india dont live in the jungle

2 have you ever visited africa asked tom

3 no but i would like to replied wes

4 what is a lions favourite meal asked sundip

5 mr simmons said that he wasnt sure

6 all the lions ive ever seen interjected tom seem to love raw meat

7 hey just look at that exclaimed mr simmons as he spotted the lions ranger bringing their food can you see all that meat

8 that should keep them well fed for a while remarked wes

9 speaking of food said sundip isnt it time we stopped for lunch

10 as he ate sundip listed all the creatures they had seen so far elephants giraffes monkeys snakes bears and of course best of all the lions

GRAMMAR

Types of sentence

There are three main types of sentence:

simple sentences
compound sentences
complex sentences

Simple sentences have one main clause and no subordinate clauses.
Example: The lions lay down to feed.

A Write a **simple** sentence about the big cats. Remember, it must only have one subject and one predicate.

Compound sentences are made up from two or more *simple sentences* joined by a conjunction, such as **and, but, or**.
Examples: **The lions / lay down to feed.** (*simple sentence*)
subject *predicate*

The vultures / sat nearby. (*simple sentence*)
subject *predicate*

The lions lay down to feed **and** the vultures sat nearby. (**compound sentence**)

B Write a second simple sentence. Then add it to your first sentence using *and*, *but*, or *or*, as has been done in the example.

C Make **compound sentences** from these pairs of sentences.

1 The River Nile is flooded.
Silts are left behind afterwards.

2 Lions cannot smell things very well.
They have excellent hearing.

3 This may be an African lion.
It may be an Asian one.

Compound sentences, made by joining two *simple sentences*, have two **main** clauses.

Female lion

A **clause** is a part of a sentence which has a proper verb.

D Copy these sentences and use a ruler to underline the two **main** clauses. Draw a circle round the conjunction (which is part of the second clause).

1 There are some lions left in Asia, but they are found only in north-west India.

2 All cats were worshipped in Egypt, and lions were particularly sacred.

3 Lions are very efficient hunters but they need to be protected from humans.

SPELLING

Another thirty tricky words

Look
Cover
Remember
Write
Check

A Here are another 30 words that frequently cause spelling difficulties. Use your dictionary to complete them correctly.

1	maint_nance	2	cat_ _pill_r	3	vacu _m
4	ras_berry	5	auxil_ary	6	independ_nce
7	hyg_enic	8	mis_letoe	9	par_ _lel
10	asp_rin	11	rest_ _ _ _nt	12	Feb_uary
13	ex_aust	14	ex_ibition	15	su_table
16	defin_te	17	a_quire	18	mess_nger
19	inten_ion	20	ph_sical	21	bound_ry
22	in_ident	23	ma_ntain	24	thor_ _gh
25	plag_e	26	leag_e	27	di_aster
28	milit_ry	29	squi_rel	30	pos_pone

QUIZ

A word cattery

You may need a dictionary to help you identify all ten **cat** words in the cattery. The first is done to help you. (**1** = catapult.)

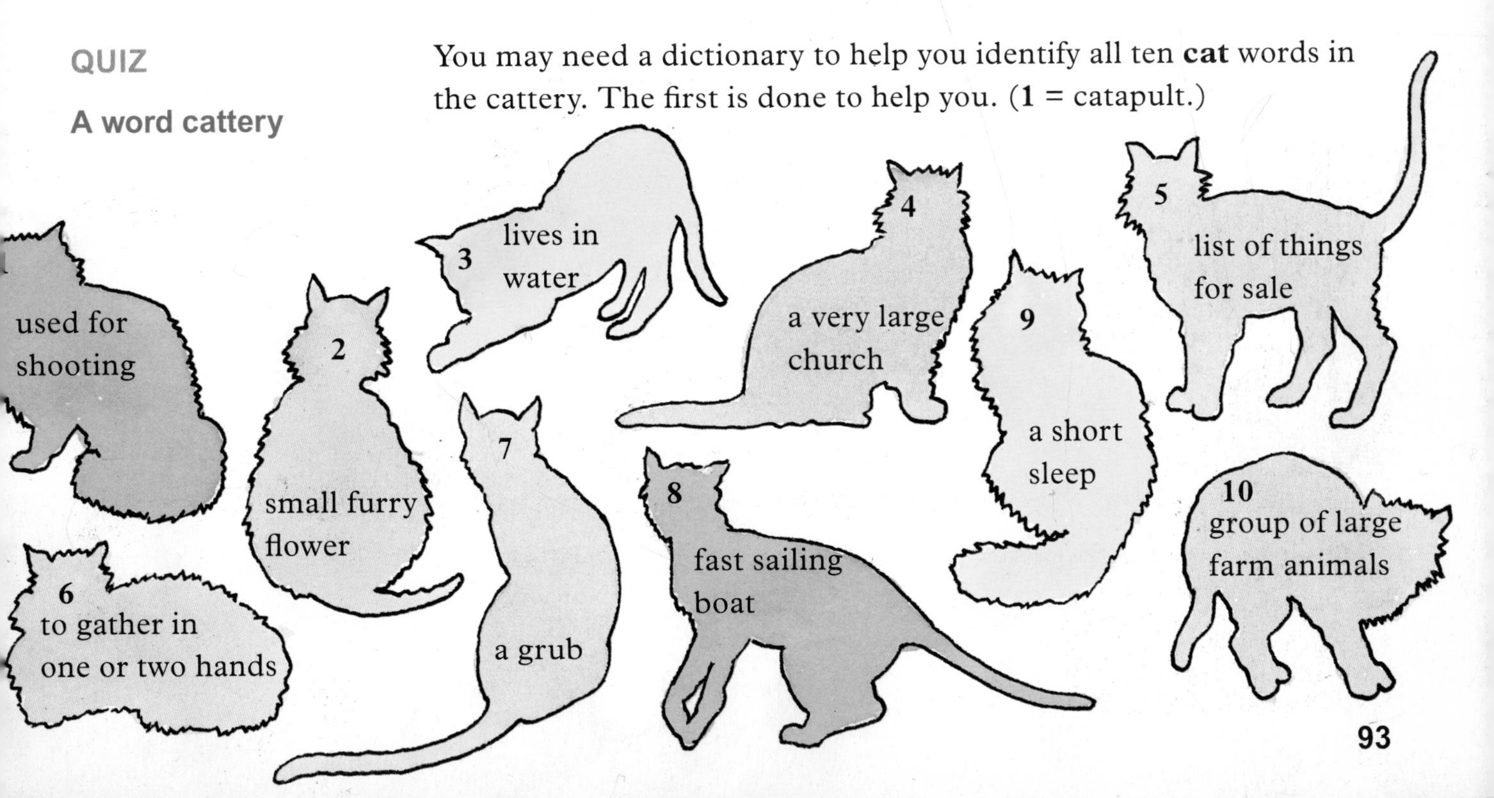

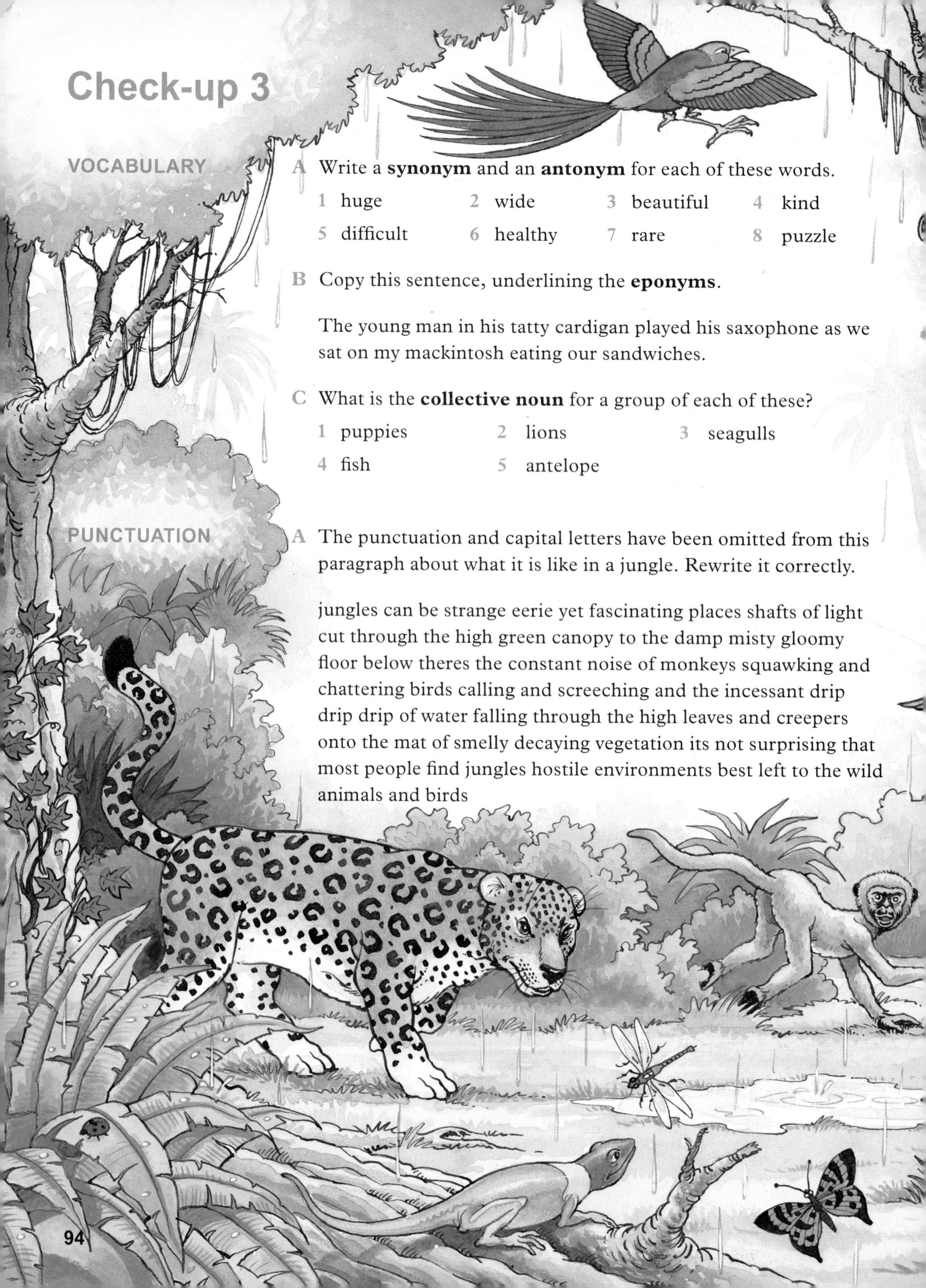

Check-up 3

VOCABULARY

A Write a **synonym** and an **antonym** for each of these words.

1 huge 2 wide 3 beautiful 4 kind
5 difficult 6 healthy 7 rare 8 puzzle

B Copy this sentence, underlining the **eponyms**.

The young man in his tatty cardigan played his saxophone as we sat on my mackintosh eating our sandwiches.

C What is the **collective noun** for a group of each of these?

1 puppies 2 lions 3 seagulls
4 fish 5 antelope

PUNCTUATION

A The punctuation and capital letters have been omitted from this paragraph about what it is like in a jungle. Rewrite it correctly.

jungles can be strange eerie yet fascinating places shafts of light cut through the high green canopy to the damp misty gloomy floor below theres the constant noise of monkeys squawking and chattering birds calling and screeching and the incessant drip drip drip of water falling through the high leaves and creepers onto the mat of smelly decaying vegetation its not surprising that most people find jungles hostile environments best left to the wild animals and birds

B Rewrite this conversation, adding the inverted commas and other punctuation, and capital letters where required. Remember to start a new line when a new person begins to speak.

do you realise enquired anita that there are over seventy countries in the world with some jungle areas i'm surprised there are that many replied mark i thought all the rainforests were being destroyed yes youre right she said unfortunately a space large enough for 60 football pitches is cleared every minute once the rainforest area was very much larger than it is today its a terrible problem

C Write a formal letter to the manager of a zoo or wildlife park that you have visited recently (pretend if necessary!), either complaining about the conditions in which the animals are housed, or congratulating him or her on the manner in which the creatures are kept.

GRAMMAR

A Choose the correct verb for each of these sentences.

1. The cheetah *run/ran* through the grass.
2. In the tree three monkeys were *sat/sitting* enjoying the shade.
3. At the waterhole antelope *drank/drunk* from the muddy pool.
4. It had *began/begun* to get dark.
5. We had *taken/took* many pictures of the animals.
6. We *was/were* all ready for a good meal.

B Improve these sentences by expanding them with words, phrases or clauses.

1. The lion had three cubs.
2. Animals gathered at the waterhole.
3. The guide took them through the jungle.

C Improve these sentences by avoiding the use of *nice*, *lot*, *bit* and *got*.

1. We got a bit of a fright when we heard the howl.
2. The lot of us got in the minibus.
3. We soon realised the animals were nice, but you had got to be a bit careful.
4. The nice old lady got lots of mosquito bites.

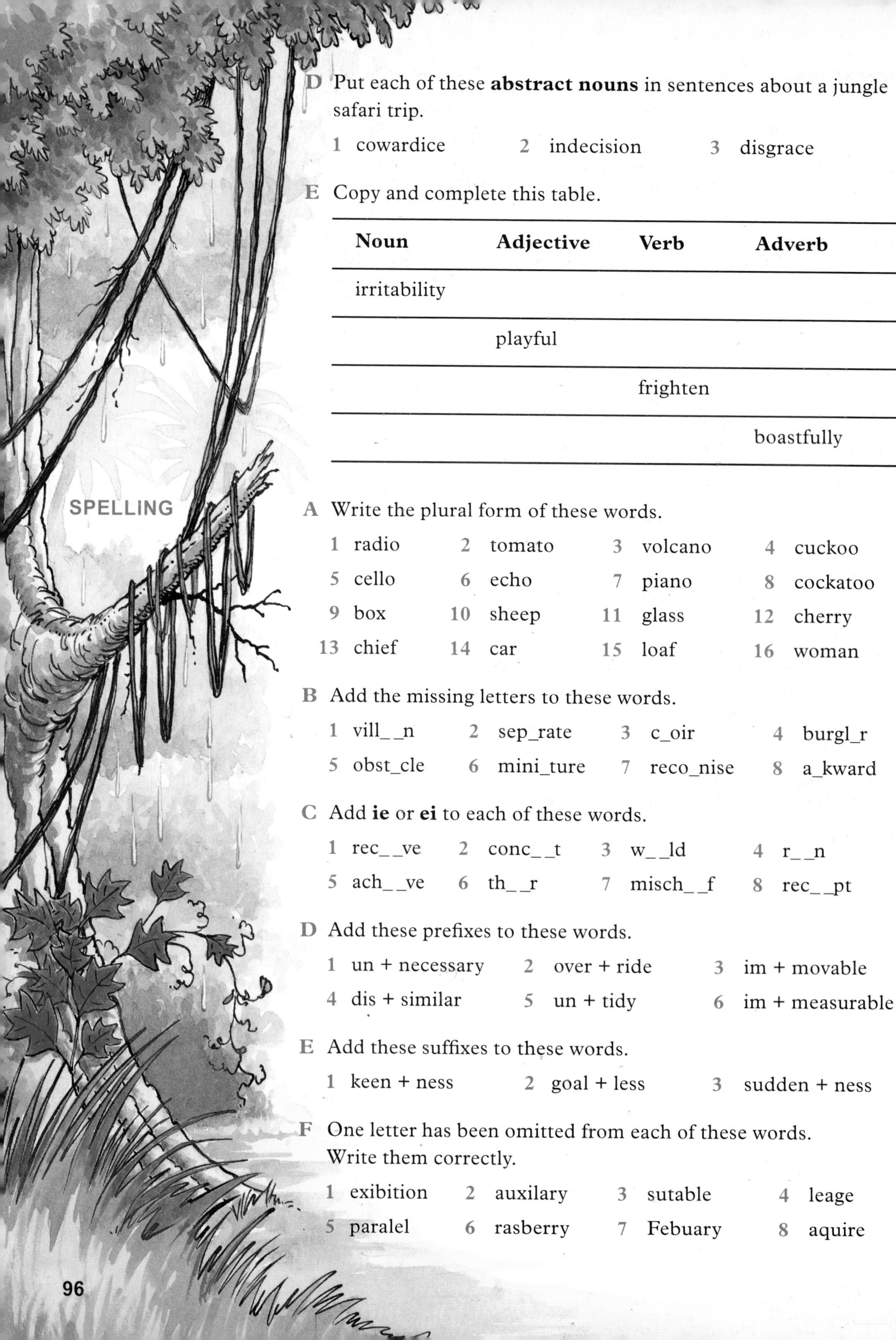

D Put each of these **abstract nouns** in sentences about a jungle safari trip.

1 cowardice 2 indecision 3 disgrace

E Copy and complete this table.

Noun	Adjective	Verb	Adverb
irritability			
	playful		
		frighten	
			boastfully

SPELLING

A Write the plural form of these words.

1 radio 2 tomato 3 volcano 4 cuckoo
5 cello 6 echo 7 piano 8 cockatoo
9 box 10 sheep 11 glass 12 cherry
13 chief 14 car 15 loaf 16 woman

B Add the missing letters to these words.

1 vill_ _n 2 sep_rate 3 c_oir 4 burgl_r
5 obst_cle 6 mini_ture 7 reco_nise 8 a_kward

C Add **ie** or **ei** to each of these words.

1 rec_ _ve 2 conc_ _t 3 w_ _ld 4 r_ _n
5 ach_ _ve 6 th_ _r 7 misch_ _f 8 rec_ _pt

D Add these prefixes to these words.

1 un + necessary 2 over + ride 3 im + movable
4 dis + similar 5 un + tidy 6 im + measurable

E Add these suffixes to these words.

1 keen + ness 2 goal + less 3 sudden + ness

F One letter has been omitted from each of these words. Write them correctly.

1 exibition 2 auxilary 3 sutable 4 leage
5 paralel 6 rasberry 7 Febuary 8 aquire